STUDIES IN COMPARATIVE EDUCATION

# LEARNING TO LIVE TOGETHER:

## BUILDING SKILLS, VALUES AND ATTITUDES FOR THE TWENTY-FIRST CENTURY

*Margaret Sinclair*

INTERNATIONAL BUREAU OF EDUCATION

The ideas and opinions expressed in this work are those of the author and do not necessarily represent the views of the UNESCO International Bureau of Education. The designations employed and the presentation of the material in this publication do not imply the expression of any opinion whatsoever on the part of the UNESCO International Bureau of Education concerning the legal status of any country, city or area or of its authorities, or concerning the delimitation of its frontiers or boundaries.

Published by the United Nations Educational, Scientific
and Cultural Organization,
7, place de Fontenoy, 75352 Paris 07 SP, France

ISBN : 92-3-103970-9

Printed by Typhon, Annecy, France

# Acknowledgements

Thanks are due especially to my colleagues Pamela Baxter, Chris Talbot, Jennifer Ashton and Nemia Temporal, who built up the UNHCR peace and life-skills education programme, which is an inspiration for this study, and to its field staff for their dedicated efforts. Thanks are due likewise to Cecilia Braslavsky, Director of the International Bureau of Education, Mary Joy Pigozzi, Director of the Division for the Promotion of Educational Quality, and Asghar Husain, Director of the Division of Educational Policies and Strategies at UNESCO Headquarters, for their kind interest, and to Sobhi Tawil for his wise guidance and support. The encouragement of my husband and children is much appreciated.

MARGARET SINCLAIR

# Table of contents

# Preface

This study represents an attempt to interpret the aim of 'learning to live together' as a synthesis of many related goals, such as education for peace, human rights, citizenship and health-preserving behaviours. It focuses specifically on the skills, values, attitudes and concepts needed for learning to live together, rather than on 'knowledge' objectives. The aim of the study is to discover 'what works' in terms of helping students learn to become politely assertive rather than violent, to understand conflict and its prevention, to become mediators, to respect human rights, to become active and responsible members of their communities—as local, national and global citizens, to have balanced relationships with others and neither to coerce others nor be coerced, especially into risky health behaviours.

Educators must be more explicit about the objectives of educational programmes in relation to these goals. There is a tendency to think that, with a bit of encouragement, teachers can handle such matters spontaneously as part of their daily teaching. But the present study shows that these goals can only be addressed successfully under special conditions. According to the findings identified by Margaret Sinclair, success is found to be associated with:

- Clearly labelled special lessons (supportive of peace, respect for human rights, active citizenship, preventive health) following a cyclic curriculum throughout the period of schooling;
- Special earmarked lesson time of not less than one period per week;
- Teachers specially trained to use experiential methods;
- Special structured teaching/learning resources designed according to pedagogic principles of sequencing and methodology.

The various goals requiring this approach need to be addressed within a co-ordinated framework, so that the cluster of behavioural skills, values and messages for conflict resolution/human rights/citizenship/preventive health are developed systematically over the years of schooling, and through non-formal studies for youth and adults.

The focus in the present study is mainly on schools. This approach has been adopted to keep the text within a reasonable length. However, much of what is said is also applicable to non-formal education for youth and adults.

The mini-case studies are mostly from post-conflict and transition situations, with which the author is more familiar, but the issues raised are applicable to the design of educational programmes more generally.

The recommendation emerging from the study for national policy-makers and curriculum specialists is that a core national team of educators committed to the goals of peace-building, human rights, active citizenship and preventive health should be created, in order to put together and pilot test materials and methodologies related to these goals. Drawing on existing national and international experience, they should seek to create a comprehensive and flexible programme within a unified framework, using 'motivational themes' identified jointly with young people as well as teachers and community leaders. The network of schools piloting this programme should be progressively expanded.

Many of the findings of the study are relevant to individual schools and to NGO education programmes. At this level also there is a need for a specially identified and resourced programme led by a core team over an extended period of time.

The study emphasizes the need for international networking to enhance our understanding of and competencies in the multi-faceted task of learning to live together, and for international support to facilitate initiatives in less-developed and at-risk countries.

Clearly, educational initiatives of the type presented here cannot bring about peace, or a well-functioning State — or an end to the HIV/AIDS epidemic. However, they can make an important contribution to such goals, complementing efforts made in other sectors.

The International Bureau of Education expresses its gratitude to Margaret Sinclair for sharing with us her extensive knowledge and experience in the domain of peace, human rights and citizenship.

CECILIA BRASLAVSKY
DIRECTOR

8

# Executive summary

1. **'Learning to live together'.**
   This represents a challenge to educators worldwide, at a time when armed conflict and violence are widespread. Many States, especially recently independent countries with ethnic or other minorities, face political instability, violence and even civil war—and education is a potential tool for peace-building. Students in all societies need to develop respect for human rights and accept the responsibilities of citizenship. They also need to learn how to resolve conflicts peacefully in their personal relationships, including negotiation and refusal skills. These skills will help protect them against health risks, such as infection with HIV/AIDS.

2. **Multiple overlapping goals and objectives.**
   Learning to live together thus entails multiple goals. The present study examines educational programmes focused on goals, such as peace and conflict resolution, social cohesion, respect for human rights and humanitarian norms, gender equality, active citizenship, environmental sustainability, and the practice of health-preserving behaviours, including HIV/AIDS prevention. Most case studies presented here encompass several of these goals. There is likewise considerable overlap of educational objectives, such as learning the skills, attitudes and values needed for co-operative problem-solving, negotiation and conflict resolution, empathy, avoidance of prejudice and bias, respect for diversity, commitment to human rights values and standards, refusal skills, a concern for the health and well-being of fellow citizens, etc. In view of the overlapping goals and objectives, it is suggested that a unified framework is required.

3. **The need for special teaching/learning methods and goal-related content.**
   This unified framework will have to take account of the learning processes required for the development of cognitive and affective skills and values. Structured experiential activities are needed to involve students actively in thinking about and developing their own values, while skills practice is

required for them to apply what they have learned. These activities take time and skilled facilitation by teachers.

4. **Case studies.**
Case studies are presented of selected programmes that have addressed some of the goals of learning to live together and that have been the subject of evaluations in the public domain.[1] They show that students can develop skills and commitments to peace, human rights, active citizenship and health-preserving behaviours. Some of the case studies focus mainly on skills and values, while others also include a knowledge component related to human rights and citizenship or preventive health.[2]

5. **Lessons learned: building a unified curriculum framework.**
The case-study programmes each focused on a particular goal or cluster of goals, but their content was found to have considerable overlap. A unified curriculum framework is needed, in which these goals feature as part of a pedagogically-derived curriculum framework for the skills and values dimensions of learning to live together. This framework should follow the principles of a cyclic (spiral) curriculum, in order to provide reinforcement and deepening of the skills and understandings acquired and of personal commitments to behavioural norms. It should cover primary and secondary schooling.

6. **Lessons learned: providing special earmarked time, special teacher training and support.**
The case studies show that a special time allocation of about one period a week is needed, during which teachers provide 'stimulus activities' that involve students personally in behavioural exercises or skills practice, and then facilitate discussion of the skills, values and concepts learned. Teachers need special training and support for this work, together with structured teaching/learning materials, since it is often difficult for them to take on the role of facilitator in relation to what may be 'sensitive' topics (e.g. reconciliation with former enemies, tolerance for other cultures and ethnicities, gender issues and sexual behaviour).

7. **Lessons learned: using a 'separate subject' or 'carrier subject' approach.**
The experience of asking teachers to 'integrate' or 'infuse' these experiential activities and discussion of sensitive topics into existing subjects is often negative. A separate earmarked period is needed for effectiveness, preferably with its own title and identity. An alternative is an earmarked period within a

'carrier subject', such as civics, social studies or moral education, with its own identity. These approaches do not consume more curriculum time than 'integration', since the development of higher-level skills and values takes time (for structured activities and guided discussion), whether included in existing subjects or treated as a subject in its own right.

8. **Lessons learned: building a core-programme development team and creating an expanding network of participating schools and teachers.**
Because of the unfamiliar methods and sensitive subject matter, it is important to build a core team of national educators, preferably people with prior commitment and skills in experiential learning. The core team can develop and pilot test locally appropriate approaches, drawing on existing national and international experience and materials, and then provide ongoing support to teachers in an expanding network of schools committed to the programme.

9. **Recommendations for action at the national level.**
The study concludes with recommendations for national curriculum renewal in this area. Some of these recommendations are relevant also to individual schools and NGO education programmes.
   (a) *Preparing to develop an integrated national framework* of education for the goals of peace, respect for human rights, active citizenship and preventive health, including HIV/AIDS prevention, through: *identifying national and regional human resources for starting up; participatory research; feasibility studies; consensus-building among stakeholders.*
   (b) Making a *strong policy commitment* and issuing a clear vision statement.
   (c) Creation of a *core development team.*
   (d) Creation of a coherent and progressive age-appropriate *unified curriculum framework* and teaching/learning materials for behavioural skills and values development related to the goals mentioned above.
   (e) Introduction of a *'separate subject'* for behavioural skills and values, with an appropriate motivational title, or series of titles, for one period a week throughout the years of schooling. If necessary, this can be an earmarked addition to an existing *'carrier'* subject. It should have its own:
   - *Special title(s);*
   - *Special time-slot in the timetable;*
   - *Special active methodology;*
   - *Special support materials based on a pedagogically sequenced curriculum;*
   - *Specially identified and specially trained teachers;*
   - *Special ongoing teacher support.*

(f) 'Integration'/'infusion' of *complementary* course units/lessons units into existing subjects.

(g) *Textbook reform* to audit and exclude elements contrary to the goals discussed here, and to include *positive modeling* of behaviours, such as mediation and conflict resolution, tolerance and non-discrimination, active citizenship, assertiveness and refusal skills in connection with preventive health, etc.

(h) *Creation and step-wise expansion of a network of participating schools* and other education institutions (pre-school, vocational, non-formal, higher education).

(i) Workshops on 'learning to live together'/conflict resolution/'life-skills'/ citizenship, etc. for *practising and trainee teachers*.

(j) Use of a *'whole school'* and *'whole community'* approach, and *multiple channels of communication*.

(k) Research, monitoring and evaluation.

10. **Recommendations for action at the international level.**

(a) Development of a *shared and inclusive discourse* on curricula for learning to live together, among actors in the fields of education for peace and conflict resolution, respect for human rights and responsibilities, local and global citizenship and preventive health, including sexual health.

(b) *Development of pedagogically-sequenced generic teaching/learning materials for schools, and other education institutions, and for the training of teachers implementing the programme.*[3]

(c) *Development of exemplar skills-based workshops* on goals in the field of 'learning to live together' for *in-service* and *pre-service teacher training*, based on experiential approaches.

(d) Building expertise in *research and evaluation* in this area.

(e) Sponsoring innovative programmes:

• Identifying and supporting *existing initiatives* in various continents/regions on an action-research basis, notably where there is an interest in *expanding the programme to cover the range of goals discussed here*, and in formative evaluation.

• Identifying governments that have an interest in moving forward in this area, and supporting *capacity-building for local development and ownership of high-impact approaches*.

• Creating a pool of *international resource persons* through special training programmes that upgrade national staff active in this field to the level of 'International Master Trainer'.

(f) Strengthening *international networking* between practitioners specializing in overlapping goals and educational objectives relating to peace, human rights, local and global citizenship, including environmental sustainability, and preventive health, including HIV/AIDS prevention.

## NOTES

1. Refugee Council Human Rights Education project in the Caucasus; the Training of Teachers in Human Rights and Democracy project in Kosovo; the Exploring Humanitarian Law programme; UNICEF's Global Education initiatives; experimental civics education in Romania; and the Escuela Nueva movement based in Colombia.
2. Experiences in HIV/AIDS education provide further insight into the difficulties of combining skills and values objectives with a knowledge component, in this case an understanding of the science of the human immunodeficiency virus.
3. Including exemplar skills and values-based workshops suited to students in vocational/technical, non-formal and higher education, and 'stand-alone' courses suited to youth and community groups. The terms 'generic' and 'exemplar' are used here to convey that the prototype materials and procedures need adaptation to students' own national and local situations and cultures. (For example: national professionals become acquainted with the generic or exemplar materials and approaches, use these approaches with national participants, and then develop and elicit nationally or locally appropriate methodologies and materials.)

# CHAPTER I
# Learning to live together
# in the twenty-first century

At the beginning of the new millennium, the challenge of learning to live together in reasonable peace and harmony preoccupies men and women of goodwill, including educators. A first concern is the multiplicity of armed conflicts across the world and the task of education for peace. Many States, especially recently independent countries with ethnic or other minorities, continue to face political instability, violence and even civil war. Problems in establishing a stable system of democratic governance, respect for human rights and the rule of law create the conditions for violent conflict. Resource shortages, such as scarcity of fresh water, are expected to worsen and generate 'environmental' conflict within and between nations and regional groupings in the future; much work is needed to build support for environmentally sustainable development. The so-called 'clash of civilizations' inspires religious traditionalists to violence across and within national boundaries, and the failure to reduce inequalities of living standards makes this danger more acute. Accelerating globalization has the potential for making these inequalities better or worse.

A second concern of educators at the present time is helping young people to take up their duties as citizens. In some countries, the opportunity for civic participation in a pluralistic society is new and the idea of tolerating different points of view and working together across political, cultural and ethnic boundaries has to be learned. Meanwhile, in the 'older democracies', there is concern that young people neglect their duties as citizens, such as voting in national and local elections and undertaking voluntary service.

Other challenges for educators at the beginning of the twenty-first century relate to students' behaviours in their personal lives. How can young people gain the skills to prevent and resolve inter-personal conflicts without resorting to violence or succumbing to abusive pressure from peers or partners? How can we help young people to become responsible and caring citizens, with respect for life and human dignity, and acting to protect the health of others as well as themselves? In some countries the priority concern is HIV/AIDS, which can best be prevented through educating young people on how to resist the pressure for unwanted or unprotected sex, education which has to impact on local behaviour patterns and pressures that put young people at risk. In every country there is concern over the use of harmful drugs by youth, much of it the result of peer influence and pressure. Worldwide, the rapid pace of social change creates a 'generation gap' between children and their parents and grandparents, creating potentially conflictual situations, and challenging educators to educate children in the skills of conflict prevention and resolution. In Western societies, moreover, many children see their parents separate and face the often conflictual relationship with step-parents and step-siblings. There continue to be serious problems of racism and bullying in schools, as well as in the wider society, and many schools fail to prepare children to cope with these pressures.[1]

The present study addresses education's role in helping us learn to live together, one of the key goals identified by the International Commission on Education for the Twenty-first Century.[2]

---

**Goals identified by the International Commission on Education for the Twenty-first Century chaired by Jacques Delors.**

The Commission identified four key objectives: learning to learn, learning to be, learning to do, and learning to live together.
*Learning to live together, learning to live with others. This type of learning is probably one of the major issues in education today* (Delors et al., 1996, p. 91).

---

## KEY QUESTIONS

Key questions to be considered include:

- Can the next generation of young people be given the skills and values to support *the non-violent resolution of conflicts at personal, school and community level*, linked to *respect for human rights* and a commitment to *civic participation*?
- Can education help build these skills and values in a way that will contribute to a *more peaceful world*, and to more just, participative and effective systems of *national and international governance*?
- Can education help young people learn to establish respectful and non-pressured relationships that take account of the danger of *sexually transmitted diseases, substance abuse and other risks to health*?

The international community believes that the answer to these questions is 'Yes', and has set itself targets for achieving 'Education for All' that incorporate these objectives. At the World Education Forum held in Dakar in April 2000, governments and other organizations pledged themselves to education promoting peace and tolerance, and providing young people with the 'life skills' to avoid health risks such as HIV/AIDS.

---

**Dakar 'Framework for Action', April 2000**

At the World Education Forum, governments agreed that the goals for quality education should include meeting twenty-first century challenges:
*We hereby collectively commit ourselves to the attainment of the following goals:*
*Goal (iii) Ensuring that the learning needs of all young people and adults are met through equitable access to appropriate learning and **life-skills** programmes;*
*Goal (vi) Improving all aspects of the quality of education and ensuring excellence of all so that recognized and measurable learning outcomes are achieved by all, especially literacy, numeracy, and **essential life-skills** [...]*
*[and] pledge ourselves to:*
*[...] (v) meet the needs of education systems affected by conflict, natural calamities and instability and conduct educational programmes in ways that promote **mutual understanding, peace and tolerance**, and that help to **prevent violence and conflict** (WEF, 2000a; emphasis added).*

---

There has been much debate about the meaning of the phrase 'life-skills' as used in Dakar Goals (iii) and (vi). The term appears to have been used in an informal way rather than as a technical term. In Goal (vi) it appears to cover everything except literacy and numeracy (although others sometimes refer to literacy and numeracy as life-skills). Many educators, especially those involved with preventive health, use 'life-skills' to mean inter-personal and intra-personal skills, as will become evident later in this study.[3]

The Dakar goals shown above are not new; they have been specified or implied in numerous international agreements and declarations. For example, the *1989 Convention on the Rights of the Child*, ratified by almost every country in the world, requires signatory governments to provide education that is supportive of peace, human rights, and responsible citizenship (Article 29), as well as education for health (Article 24) and for protection from substance abuse (Article 33).[4]

---

**Education for peace and human rights under the Convention on the Rights of the Child (1989)**

*States Parties agree that the education of the child shall be directed to:*
*[...]*
*(b) The development of respect for human rights and fundamental freedoms [...]*
*(c) The development of respect for [...] the national values of the country in which the child is living, the country from which he or she may originate, and for civilizations different from his or her own;*
*(d) The preparation of the child for responsible life in a free society, in the spirit of understanding, peace, tolerance, equality of sexes and friendship among all peoples, ethnic, national and religious groups and persons of indigenous origin.*
*(e) The development of respect for the natural environment. (Article 29)*

---

## RESPONDING TO THE CHALLENGES

In the following pages, we shall examine some of the responses that the education community has developed in recent years to meet the challenges noted above. Case studies are presented, covering programmes focused on education for peace and tolerance, respect for human rights and humanitarian norms, active citizenship and preventive health behaviours. The studies draw especially on the experience of communities and countries at risk of conflict or in post-conflict situations, in political transition, and/or at risk of HIV/AIDS. However, many of the lessons learned are of more general application, and will face educators in any country who address the sensitive issues of personal behaviour, and local and global citizenship.

The case studies were selected to illustrate a range of approaches and were prioritized as having been the subject of some form of external evaluation. They show that positive results have been obtained in programmes that have used interactive and experiential approaches, and that have allocated the curricular time required for this, together with providing extensive teacher support.

Attention in the study has been focused mainly on schools, because of their outreach to such a large proportion of children and young people. Much of the discussion that follows applies also to non-formal education, where there are many initiatives in this area, often on a small scale and not well documented. The present analysis is relevant likewise to vocational, higher and teacher-education institutions. To explore this broader canvas would be a major task, but it is to be hoped that educational researchers will undertake this review in the near future.

The present study includes:

- A review of some of the multiple and overlapping challenges facing educators in areas from conflict prevention to promoting active citizenship and health-promoting behaviours, with a focus on the extensive overlap between their goals and objectives.
- A review of the educational principles underlying the development of skills and values oriented to conflict prevention and resolution, respect for human rights, active citizenship and responsible relationships.
- Illustrations of programmes that focus heavily on learning, practising and internalizing behavioural skills and values needed for:
  - —— conflict resolution, mediation, promotion of tolerance, peace, reconciliation;
  - —— 'life skills' that help young people cope with peer pressure and avoid risky behaviours, including exposure to HIV/AIDS;
  - —— respect for human rights and humanitarian norms;
  - —— active and responsible citizenship.
- Lessons learned regarding:
  - —— programme goals and their inter-relatedness;
  - —— the teaching/learning process;
  - —— 'separate subject' and other approaches;
  - —— the process of innovation;
- Suggested features of a high-impact model.
- Suggestions for international support.

**The recommendation emerging from this study is to allocate earmarked curriculum time for structured educational activities to build skills and values needed for conflict resolution, respect for human rights, active citizenship and preventive health, using participative experiential approaches and facilitated discussion and reflection, led by specially trained teachers.** The study shows that these are the preconditions for effective impact on the skills development, value orientations and attitudinal changes needed for positive behavioural learning outcomes, for learning to live together.

NOTES

1. For a broader view of twenty-first century educational challenges see, for example, UNESCO (1996), Dalin (1998).
2. Poverty reduction is not addressed directly in this study. However, the poorest countries include many that have suffered from civil conflict, so programmes focused

on education for peace and citizenship are among the best investments for poverty reduction. A second point is that the interpersonal and decision-making skills central to education for peace, human rights, active citizenship and preventive health are also of great importance in the world of work. Many of the same communications and negotiation exercises are found in high-level management training courses.

3.  In this case, vocational skills are given the separate title of 'livelihood skills', which perhaps vary more with local conditions than core inter-personal and intra-personal skills. Practical skills like changing a torch battery, filling in a form or reading a map are sometimes called life-skills, but from the educational viewpoint may be seen as applications of normal school subjects, such as science, languages or social sciences respectively.

4.  The term 'life-skills' was not used in the Convention, having come to the fore at the international level more recently, especially in connection with education for HIV/AIDS prevention.

CHAPTER II
# Educational responses:
# multiple titles, overlapping goals

There have been and continue to be many educational initiatives designed to help people live together in peace and with respect for the human dignity and well-being of others. We may begin our analysis by noting that it is hard to find a single name for these initiatives and their goals — to find a single word or phrase that adequately embraces the goals of conflict prevention and resolution, tolerance, respect for cultural and ethnic diversity, gender sensitivity, civic participation, non-abusive relationships, respect for the health of one's fellows and of the environment. Some people bring these goals together under the term 'positive peace'[1] or as a pillar of sustainable development. Others see them all as supporting human rights. UNESCO speaks of 'learning to live together' or of 'education for universal values', referring to behavioural norms accepted 'universally' by the international community through nations' adherence to various international declarations and conventions.

It will be argued later that these goals share many specific educational objectives, such as the practical application of cognitive and inter-personal skills to effective and considerate communication; perception that is self-aware and not prejudiced; analysis of the consequences of one's actions; co-operative problem-solving; negotiation and mediation; in the context of empathy, active and responsible citizenship, peace, human dignity and well-being. They also share some knowledge and conceptual objectives (e.g. in relation to human rights). The logical consequence of these shared objectives, given the already heavy pressures on school timetables, is for the goals to be approached in a coordinated manner. This does not mean, however, that the motivational force of each deeply felt problem, and the goal of contributing through education to its solution, should be sacrificed. In any given situation, problem-oriented education initiatives need titles that are acceptable to and motivate policy makers, teachers, students and their families. *Since the aim is behaviour change, including adoption of pro-social*

*values, the motivational force of the title or titles is of importance in itself.* [2]
Educational initiatives in this area can be categorized by the types of goals they set out to achieve:

TABLE 1: **Educational initiatives for learning to live together**

| Educational initiative | Nature of learning goals [3] |
|---|---|
| Peace education | Conflict resolution, peace, reconciliation, tolerance, respect for human rights, civic participation... |
| Education for mutual understanding | Social cohesion, respect for diversity, inclusive national identity... |
| Multicultural/intercultural education | Tolerance, respect for diversity, anti-racism, non-discrimination... |
| Human rights education | Respect for human rights and responsibilities, rights of women, children and minorities, tolerance, non-discrimination, prevention of bullying, civic participation... |
| Life-skills'/ health education | Preventive health/HIV-AIDS prevention, prevention of substance abuse, respect for the health rights of others, respectful relationships... |
| Citizenship education | Active and responsible participation in civic/political life, democracy, respect for human rights, tolerance... |
| Education for sustainable development | Environmental sustainability, respect for the rights and welfare of all... |
| Humanitarian education | Respect for humanitarian norms, humanitarian acts, non-discrimination... |
| Values education | Internalization of values of peace, respect and concern for others..... |

While the educational initiatives listed above have different titles that reflect different motivational starting points, these initiatives clearly have overlapping goals. This will become evident as we examine some of the programme areas below.

## PEACE EDUCATION: GOALS RELATED TO CONFLICT RESOLUTION, PEACE, RECONCILIATION, TOLERANCE, RESPECT FOR HUMAN RIGHTS, CIVIC PARTICIPATION...

**The foundations of peace**

*Since wars begin in the minds of men, it is in the minds of men that the defences of peace should be constructed.*

(Preamble of UNESCO Constitution, 1946)

There have been numerous attempts by international agencies, governments and NGOs to develop education programmes that are specifically supportive of the goals of peace, co-existence, conflict resolution and reconciliation, especially in conflict-affected societies.[4] UNICEF, for example, has supported governments and NGOs undertaking peace-education initiatives in Lebanon, Sri Lanka, Burundi, Liberia, and many other countries (Fountain, 1997, 1999; UNICEF, 2000).[5, 6] UNESCO has worked to promote peace education worldwide,[7] including programmes under adverse conditions in Somalia.[8] The Office of the United Nations High Commissioner for Refugees (UNHCR), working jointly with its NGO or governmental partners, has developed a peace and 'life-skills' programme used in various refugee and post-conflict situations.[9] Many NGOs specialising in peace-building at community or national level have also undertaken peace-education activities. For example, the International Federation for Reconciliation provides training of trainers in many countries, as does the Center for Non-violent Communication.[10, 11]

These initiatives often incorporate curriculum objectives of developing skills and values for peaceful and respectful behaviours at the level of individual students and their peers and families, alongside objectives of promoting the values of peace and tolerance at community and national levels. Skills-based peace-education programmes seek to introduce students to the skills of respectful two-way communication, avoiding prejudice, appropriate assertiveness, creative problem-solving, negotiation, mediation and reconciliation. Through experiential approaches and participative discussion linked to students' values frameworks, these programmes aim to build and internalize behaviours that will prevent or resolve conflict. These activities take time and teacher skills, as noted in later chapters.

Special factors may arise during and after civil conflict that make the objectives controversial, such as the 'collision between two contradicting, deeply rooted collective narratives', 'collectively-held beliefs about "us" and about "them"', built-in inequalities, strong emotions and a context of 'animosity, fear and belligerence' (Salomon, 2003). When these factors are present, the task of preparing teachers for peace education is more complex and requires greater resources.

---

**Divergent meanings of peace education**

*Peace education has many divergent meanings for different individuals in different places. For some, peace education is mainly a matter of changing mindsets: the general purpose is to promote understanding, respect and tolerance for yesterday's neighbours [...] in regions of intractable conflict such as Northern Ireland, Israel or Bosnia. For others, peace education is mainly a matter of cultivating a set of skills [...] to acquire a non-violent disposition and conflict resolution skills [in] school violence programmes, peer mediation, and conflict-resolution programmes. For still others, particularly in Third World countries, peace education is mainly a matter of promoting human rights, while in more affluent countries it is often a matter of environmentalism, disarmament and the promotion of a culture of peace.'[12]*

---

Depending on the context, peace education may or may not incorporate extensive knowledge objectives, beyond building a deeper understanding of the core skills, norms and values for living together in peace.

Where circumstances and resources permit and especially for older students, a broader set of themes may be included in the programme. Betty Reardon and Alicia Cabezudo (2002) have suggested a framework for peace education, oriented mainly to education at secondary and higher education levels, incorporating a knowledge framework based on the 1999 *Hague Agenda for Peace and Justice for the Twenty First Century*.[13] The framework comprises:

- roots of war/culture of peace
- international humanitarian and human rights law and institutions
- prevention, resolution and transformation of violent conflict
- disarmament and human security.

Reardon and Cabezudo emphasize the values of non-violence and social justice, suggesting that 'a value such as non-violence is manifested through other values such as respect for human rights, freedom, and trust, while social justice is realized by values such as equality, responsibility and solidarity'.[14] Peace education must include awareness of the dilemmas regarding violence, however — that apparent submissiveness may invite aggression, and that even peace-keepers need the capability to protect civilians from attack. Students should be helped to realize for themselves the core value of minimizing the use of violence.[15]

The goals of 'peace education' can perhaps be seen on a spectrum, ranging from the focus on core behavioural skills and values — when the situation is far from peaceful, as in a post-conflict situation filled with mistrust and danger, to a mix of these core objectives with understanding of internationally agreed human rights — when the situation is a little more secure; and with the further objective of preparation for active citizenship — when there is a clear path forward to a free pluralistic society.

## EDUCATION FOR MUTUAL UNDERSTANDING: GOALS OF SOCIAL COHESION, RESPECT FOR DIVERSITY, INCLUSIVE NATIONAL IDENTITY...

Many countries that have not experienced civil war are nevertheless *at risk of* conflict and discrimination between different sectors of the population and need education for conflict prevention, peace and mutual respect. In this case the goal may be expressed as social cohesion, respect for diversity or 'learning to live together'. This theme was discussed by the world's Education Ministers at the International Conference on Education in 2001 (UNESCO, 2001; UNESCO, 2003b). An earlier sub-regional seminar in the Caribbean illustrated the presence of this goal in the education policy statements and social studies curricula of many countries: 'to promote brotherhood among Dominicans', 'developing skills needed for communal, national and world harmony' (Jamaica), promoting 'an appreciation of and respect for different people and cultures' (Belize). The seminar report notes the difficulty of achieving these objectives within existing school programmes (Byron and Rozemeijer, 2001).

At policy level, there has been discussion of education for social cohesion, especially in the context of ethnic tensions[16], and the term 'respect for diversity' is sometimes used as a more inspirational phrase targeting the same goal.[17] The UNESCO International Bureau of Education has worked with curriculum specialists from conflict-affected countries to locate good practice in helping students develop a pluralistic and inclusive sense of national identity.[18]

## MULTI-CULTURAL AND INTER-CULTURAL EDUCATION: GOALS OF TOLERANCE, RESPECT FOR DIVERSITY, ANTI-RACISM, NON-DISCRIMINATION...

Another set of goals focused on conflict prevention and enabling people to live more comfortably together are ideas such as 'positive tolerance', meaning the welcoming of diversity as a source of enrichment of society.[19] There is substantial overlap between activities designed to promote tolerance and those designed to promote peace and human rights.

In many Western societies there are educational movements in favour of multicultural education, designed to promote tolerance and to counter racism. Many schools enable students to learn about other cultural traditions in terms of their 'heroes and holidays', but some educators consider that multi-cultural and inter-cultural education should be more structured.[20, 21] Clear behavioural goals and structured programmes to develop the appropriate behavioural skills and values are needed to overcome the prejudice and indifference encountered by minority and foreign-born groups in many societies.[22]

TABLE 2: **Tolerance: general learning goals**

| **Values** | **Knowledge** | **Capacities and skills** |
|---|---|---|
| Human dignity/ rights | Varieties of human, personal and cultural identities, social issues | Living with diversity: cross-cultural co-operation; using human rights standards to make judgements |
| Social justice/democracy | Multiple forms of democratic processes and governance | Exercising responsibility: critical reflection; communication of facts and opinions; political decision-making |
| Co-operative non-violent society/peace | Alternative ways of responding constructively to human differences and conflicts | Managing conflict: discussion and debate; conflict resolution; reconciliation; social reconstruction; co-operative problem-solving and task achievement |

Source: Reardon, 1997:Unit 1, p.53

## HUMAN RIGHTS EDUCATION: GOALS OF RESPECT FOR HUMAN RIGHTS AND RESPONSIBILITIES, RIGHTS OF WOMEN, CHILDREN AND MINORITIES, TOLERANCE, NON-DISCRIMINATION, PREVENTION OF BULLYING, CIVIC PARTICIPATION...

Human rights education is seen by some educators as having a primary goal of helping young people develop the basic values of caring for and respecting others, non-violent conflict resolution and so on. For others the primary goal is understanding the protection of people's well-being through national and international law. Both goals are important. Thus, the 1993 World Conference on Human Rights declared that 'human rights education should include peace, democracy, development and social justice, [...] humanitarian law, [...] and rule of law'. The UN Resolution establishing the UN Decade for Human Rights Education (1995-2004) referred to learning 'respect for the dignity of others and the means and methods of ensuring that respect in all societies'.

A recent human rights education handbook (Flowers, 2000) focuses on the 1948 UN Universal Declaration of Human Rights as the heart of all human rights education because of its symbolic role, as well as its 'grand simplicity of language and inspiring vision'. The key educational objective is identified as understanding and adopting the core human rights principles of:

- Equality;
- Universality;
- Non-discrimination;
- Indivisibility of rights;
- Interdependence of rights;
- Responsibility (of governments, individuals, other entities).

The knowledge objectives suggested in the handbook include the history of human rights, the Universal Declaration, other human rights instruments, and their relationship to the national constitution and laws. The personal values and skills objectives include:

- Recognising one's own biases;
- Accepting differences;
- Respecting the rights of others;
- Taking responsibility for defending the rights of others;
- Active listening;
- Consensus-building;
- Mediation and conflict resolution.[23]

Practical skills are also seen as important, including action skills, such as advocacy, networking, lobbying and community organizing, and documentation and analysis skills.[24]

Human rights education thus overlaps substantially with education for peace, tolerance and other goals cited earlier, with their emphasis on a common humanity, the need to respect others, to avoid prejudice and to solve problems constructively. In terms of behavioural skills and values objectives, there is much in common.

*Gender sensitivity and respect for the rights of women* are principal educational goals of the twenty-first century, since rapid social change has necessitated new standards of behaviour, as set out in the *1979 Convention on the Elimination of All Forms of Discrimination Against Women* and the *1995 Beijing Declaration*.[25] Given the prevalence of gender-based, relationship-based and sexual violence, both physical and mental, in all societies, human rights education must include strong elements of gender-sensitive training for appropriate assertiveness, negotiation skills, conflict prevention and resolution, and decision-making to guard sexual, reproductive and general health and well-being. Human rights education should strengthen the ability of women to protect themselves and their children from harm, as well as encouraging and empowering the less 'macho' aspects of the other half of the population's 'masculinity'.[26, 27]

---

*Goals and methods: gender equality and sensitivity*

*Values: commitment to the equal value of women and men rooted in the value of universal human dignity. Belief that gender balance should prevail in all social institutions and human relationships based on the concept of complementarity.*

*Capacities: behaviours that provide equal opportunities and honour both the similarities and differences between men and women. Avoidance of gender stereotyping and limiting human achievement on the basis of sex. Seeking partnerships between men and women based on complementarity and mutual enhancement.*

*Skills: see issues and problems from perspectives of both men and women, boys and girls. Recognize stereotypes; observe their inaccuracies and limitations. Use of gender-inclusive language for general references to human beings. Analyse differences, similarities and complementarities in a cultural context.*

*Knowledge: knowledge of origins and formation of gender roles. Cultural variations in gender roles and perceptions of masculine and feminine. Negative consequences of devaluing or repressing one gender or privileging one –specific knowledge of oppression of women. Positive consequences of equality, mutuality, and complementarity.*

*Pedagogy: keeping journals on personal gender experiences. Readings in gender studies and women's issues. Study of women's movements and international standards on women's rights. Role plays of 'gender incidents' from both perspectives. (Reardon, 2001, p. 160-161)*

---

Betty Reardon, in her *Education for a culture of peace in a gender perspective* (2001: 158-161), lists five components: education for environmental sustainability; cultural diversity; human solidarity/justice/peace; social responsibility/human rights; and gender equality[28] — with gender elements featuring in each (see box).

Gender issues and gender sensitivity feature as educational objectives in most of the programmes discussed in the present study. It is important, however, to make them explicit, so that the message is not missed, either by teachers or students. It is important that experiential (activity-based) modules specifically focused on the goal of gender sensitivity be included in behavioural-skills and values-education programmes for schools, as well as in relevant programmes of non-formal education.[29]

The 1989 *Convention on the Rights of the Child* requires that children are taught about their rights. This would, of course, be inappropriate without children also learning about their responsibilities to ensure the rights of others. The Convention thus implies, *inter alia*, considerate and respectful relations with their peers, non-violent conflict resolution, and responsible citizenship.

A basic goal for a school management committed to the rights of the child is educating students (and teachers) to prevent *bullying, scapegoating and youth violence* generally. This is a worldwide phenomenon. Even in peaceful and prosperous Sweden, some 17% of boys and 16% of girls in grade two of schooling reported being bullied, declining with age to 6% of boys and 3% of girls in grade nine. About 10% of boys in all grades reported that they bullied other students, although the percentage of girls who reported themselves to be bullies was much less.[30] Bullying is a serious concern in other cultures, for example, Japan (Yohji, 1996). School violence and the influence of street gangs in schools is of concern in many countries from the USA (Stromquist and Vigil, 1996) to Brazil (Guimaraes, 1996) and South Africa (Fraser et al., 1996).

Bullying and harassment by students or teachers is indeed a human rights abuse, right within the social setting of a school. Anti-bullying programmes share the features of education for conflict prevention and human rights education, since students have to learn that each person matters and how to cope with aggression. The programmes must encourage students to have consideration for the rights of others and not to act as passive bystanders when the rights of others are violated.[31] They must equip potential victims with assertiveness skills and self-esteem, and enable potential bullies to control their behaviour.

## LIFE-SKILLS/HEALTH EDUCATION: GOALS OF PREVENTIVE HEALTH/HIV-AIDS PREVENTION, PREVENTION OF SUBSTANCE ABUSE, RESPECT FOR THE HEALTH RIGHTS OF OTHERS, RESPECTFUL RELATIONSHIPS ...

This type of education is typically designed to help students develop the skills and confidence to resist peer pressure to engage in risky behaviours that can lead to AIDS, drug abuse, unwanted teenage pregnancies, etc. 'Skills-based health education' and related 'life-skills' programmes have been promoted in recent years due to the failure of facts-based health education to achieve the goal of changing culturally-entrenched behaviours.[32] This has been a problem especially in relation to education about HIV/AIDS, where adolescents may learn the facts about transmission of the virus in school, but do not necessarily change their sexual expectations and risky behaviours, such as pressuring others or being pressured into unwanted or unprotected sex. Hence, there is a need for both boys and girls to learn self-respect and 'respect for the other', and to master the skills for assertiveness and negotiation.[33] Education regarding HIV/AIDS should also cover the understandings, skills and values needed for helping, rather than being prejudiced against, those who are infected; and, where needed, personal skills for living with HIV infection.

Many of the objectives sought under 'life-skills education' and 'skills-based health education' overlap with those of peace and conflict resolution, human rights and responsible citizenship. Whitman & Aldinger (2002), for example, cite the objectives: refusal of and advocacy against consumption of addictive substances; behaviour change towards and advocacy of a healthy diet; refusal of risky sexual behaviours and caring for victims of HIV/AIDS; advocacy of environmental behaviours reducing helminth (worm) infections; and violence prevention or peace education. Adolescents need conflict-management skills to be able to resist adults, peers or partners who are pressuring them to take risks with their health. Hence the emphasis in this study that *preventive-health, coping-skills and relationships education is an important component of peace and human rights education, and vice versa.*

## CITIZENSHIP EDUCATION: GOALS OF ACTIVE AND RESPONSIBLE PARTICIPATION IN CIVIC/POLITICAL LIFE, DEMOCRACY, RESPECT FOR HUMAN RIGHTS, TOLERANCE ...

Many of the goals and objectives under discussion here can be considered as elements of 'education for citizenship': for example, education for peaceful coexistence and reconciliation in a post-conflict society, and education for human rights in a society previously subject to human rights violations.[34] 'Civics', 'education for democracy' and human rights education have been to the fore in East European and other societies making the transition from one-party to multi-party systems, with the goal of promoting skills, values and behaviours needed to make such systems function well and build civil society to complement and counterbalance the power of the State.[35, 36] Education for active citizenship has likewise gained ground in Western Europe in recent years, partly because of social problems, such as youth violence and hooliganism, and partly because of low turnout in local, national and European Union elections. In Australia, civics educators aim to promote civic inclusion of all indigenous peoples and of foreign-born immigrants (22% of the population), and to affirm the notion that 'identities are multiple rather than single' as a crucial component of democracy and the sense of national identity (Kennedy & Mellor, 2000).

Citizenship education requires teachers and students to constantly move up and down these frames of reference. In a review of curriculum reforms in support of democracy in Latin America, Cox (2002, p. 122) comments on the attention given to respect for local diversity in the national curriculum of Brazil, with its many ethnic groups, as well as goals related to the nation State. He observes the attention given in the curricula of Argentina and Chile to support for the global norms of the Universal Declaration of Human Rights and other human rights instruments, noting a tendency to 'redefine the locus of the moral regulation of the political, subordinating the nation to humanity.' The goals of education for active citizenship include behaviours at the levels of the individual (tolerance, community service, voting, avoiding corrupt practices), the local community, the state and the global community.

The concept of citizenship education as incorporating the skills and values goals relating to peace, tolerance, responsible behaviours in terms of society and the environment, and laying the foundations for democratic governance, may be illustrated by Argentina's primary school curriculum, in the 'chapter' for Ethical and Citizenship Education (see box).

---

**Contents of Ethical and Citizenship Education in the 1995 National Curriculum, Argentina (grades 7, 8, 9)**

**Development of attitudes:**
- Flexibility, tolerance and respect for differences
- Co-operation and solidarity

---

- Valuing of national identity and respectful relations with other identities
- Responsible participation in the context of democratic society
- Dialogue, understanding and rational resolution of conflicts.

**Conceptual contents: values**
- Factors that condition human action
- Freedom, autonomy and responsibility
- The notion of value and its relation to the actions of persons
- Relativism, scepticism and fundamentalism [37]
- The universality of values and its relation to the dignity of persons
- Common good and personal responsibility.

**Conceptual contents: norms and society**
- Characteristics of social norms
- Differences between legal and social norms
- Norms and justice
- Norms as the recognition and guarantee of the person's dignity
- The rule of law as a basis for living together and procedure for rational conflict resolution

**Conceptual contents: human rights**
- Causes of the Declaration of Human Rights
- The need for universalizing human rights
- The need to defend the human condition against hunger, genocide, ignorance and persecution
- Civil, political, economic, social and cultural rights
- Individual, group, social and political responsibilities in the defence of human rights
- Defence of the natural environment and the issue of the historical expansion of rights
- Violence as an offence against living together
- Discrimination against women, the disabled and others as a violation of human rights
- Some stereotypes as violation of human rights.

**Conceptual contents: the national constitution**
- Historical understanding of the national constitution
- History of constitutional reforms
- History of the successive breakdowns of the constitutional order
- Democracy, organization of the state, federal organization of the nation
- Democracy as a form of socio-political organization and as a lifestyle
- Historical origins and evolution of constitutional rights
- Rights, guarantees and their relationships with duties and responsibilities
- Citizenship

**Skills or procedural objectives**
- To think in a rigorous, conscious, constructive and critical manner
- To recognize informal mistaken beliefs in discourse and formal reasoning and to distinguish different types of reasoning
- To define and analyse problems with precision
- To develop one's own creative potential in different learning areas
- To analyse concrete situations from the perspective of values.
- To begin reflecting on the foundations of customs, values, virtues and the more common norms accepted by society.
- To be prepared to act on values freely chosen according to one's own convictions and to those of one's group allegiances

**Procedural contents**
- Gathering information about typical social norms
- Searching for, collecting and setting out information about the relationship between democracy and human dignity.
- Critical analysis of situations.
- Collecting historical information
- Gathering information from different members of the community
- Analysis of present situations. (Cox, 2002: p. 110, 116)

The *'Training for democratic citizenship'* manual developed by the Council of Europe uses many of the same experiential exercises found in peace and 'life-skills' education, as a means of getting students interested in new behaviours and values. Objectives include:
- clarifying values
- getting to know human rights
- perceiving others
- making justice work
- understanding political philosophy
- taking part in politics
- dealing with conflict (COE, 2000) [38]

In South-Eastern Europe, there is a strong emphasis on the values of democracy and development of competencies for taking part in civic life, based on the central value of respect for human rights. [39, 40]

The action dimension is important in citizenship education, which can too often be descriptive and not involve the students at a personal level. Thus the education objectives of *'Project Citizen'*, developed by the Center for Civic Education in Calabasas, California, and now found in several locations outside the USA, are built around problem-solving, with four stages:

- explaining the problem;
- evaluating alternative policies to deal with the problem;
- developing a public policy the class will support;
- developing an action plan to get government to accept the class policy.[41, 42]

A thematic approach closely related to the goals considered in the present study is adopted in the new civics education curriculum in Rwanda, where key educational objectives include:
- Essential life-skills;
- Peace, unity and reconciliation;
- Human and children's rights;
- Gender balance;
- HIV/AIDS prevention;
- Environmental protection;
- Population management;
- Democratic principles and good governance;
- Participatory approaches.[43]

## EDUCATION FOR SUSTAINABLE DEVELOPMENT: GOALS OF ENVIRONMENTAL SUSTAINABILITY, RESPECT FOR THE RIGHTS AND WELFARE OF ALL ...

Education for sustainable development is a broad topic, — the subject of a United Nations Decade (2005-2014). At its heart is the goal of helping students to build responsible attitudes and behaviours in respect of the environment. Environmental issues have been mainstreamed into the teaching of science and social studies in some countries. Attention must be given, however, to the goal of motivating students to act, so far as possible, in a way that preserves the environment for themselves and their descendants, as well as coping with environmental problems in a non-conflictual and equitable manner.[44]

Environment is an area where the 'bottom-up' approach to education can balance the 'top-down' nature of much curriculum. Students can find goals for themselves in their local environment, and will see the linkages of those goals to life dimensions such as local and global citizenship, democracy and gender (Dillon & Teamey, 2002).[45]

The 'key action themes' envisaged for the Education for Sustainable Development Decade overlap substantially with the other goals under discussion here, including intercultural understanding and peace, human rights, gender equity, HIV/AIDS prevention, and respect for cultural diversity.[46]

# HUMANITARIAN EDUCATION: GOALS OF RESPECT FOR HUMANITARIAN NORMS, HUMANITARIAN ACTS, NON-DISCRIMINATION ...

Humanitarian action refers to people's initiatives in promoting human welfare, saving human lives or the alleviation of suffering, especially on a voluntary basis outside their normal family and work-place obligations. Humanitarian organizations act to help people caught up in difficulties outside their control. It is important for children and young people to be introduced to humanitarian values, and learn how to help others in distress, from the elderly house-bound in their own neighbourhoods to children forcibly recruited as child soldiers, land-mine victims and others facing unforeseen troubles elsewhere. *The humanitarian imperative is to act to help others, not merely to do no harm, and is thus central to active citizenship.*

The International Committee of the Red Cross (ICRC) has recently initiated an educational programme to introduce young people to the norms and standards of international humanitarian law, which seeks to limit suffering in times of armed conflict (Tawil, 2000). Given the many countries that have experienced or are experiencing civil conflict in which children and adolescents participate as combatants, in some instances committing atrocities, this is an important educational goal. Students should understand the horrendous consequences of armed conflict, so that they are not attracted to a false ideal of the nobility of modern war. Moreover, people worldwide should be aware of the Geneva Conventions and their implications for related issues such as ensuring correct behaviour by troops serving on international peace-keeping missions. Humanitarian and human rights education overlap substantially and if both areas are tackled by students the results are likely to be more deep-seated. The many examples of heroic humanitarian behaviour in the ICRC course, for example, can be inspirational to young people.

It is important that humanitarian action and international norms regarding constraints on armed conflict are included in the mix of themes presented during the years of schooling, as well as by non-formal and informal education channels. The Red Cross and Red Crescent Movement can provide valuable support to both formal and non-formal education in humanitarian norms and in combating discrimination (Tawil & Azami-Tawil, 2001).

## VALUES EDUCATION: INTERNALIZATION OF VALUES OF PEACE, RESPECT AND CONCERN FOR OTHERS ...

The goals cited above share the common aim of encouraging pro-social behaviour requiring attitudes and values such as respect and concern for others, co-operation and taking responsibility for oneself and one's society.[47] They are based at root on values of a personal nature. There is thus substantial overlap with the objectives of 'values education' programmes, such as the Living Values initiative, which focuses on peace, respect, love, tolerance, happiness, responsibility, co-operation, humility, simplicity, freedom, and unity. The various goals imply a commitment to the instrumental norms and values developed at national and international level such as respect for human rights and humanitarian law, responsible civic participation, democracy and the rule of law.[48] A values education programme developed recently in the Asian and Pacific region includes values at both personal and societal levels: health and harmony with nature, truth and wisdom, love and compassion, creativity and appreciation of beauty, peace and justice, sustainable human development, national unity and global solidarity, and global spirituality (UNESCO, 2002b).[49]

It may be noted that the various themes under discussion in this study represent a good vehicle for reinsertion of values into school programmes that some observers perceive as having become too focused on cognitive objectives and preparation for employment. In Australia, for example, there has been a movement to reintroduce values in the curriculum (Hill, 1998), while a major survey was undertaken in Europe to identify values underlying school curricula (Taylor, 1993).[50, 51] 'Values education' as such can be controversial in certain settings — as when there is heavy ideological or nationalist emphasis. However, educators in such settings may have the option of introducing core values through one of the other themes discussed above.

---

**Values considered important in education, Europe**

Key topics cited in a 1993 survey of values considered important for education in Eastern and Western Europe were environmental awareness (fourteen countries), inter-cultural/multi-cultural education (twelve), international understanding (twelve), citizenship (twelve), democracy (eleven), peace (eleven), anti-racism (ten), tolerance (six), national consciousness (six), human rights (five), gender equality (five), social justice (four), anti-violence (four), various health education themes (a few West European countries) and sixteen topics nominated by three or less countries. (Taylor, 1993, p. 44-47)

---

National curricular frameworks now tend to specify desired educational outcomes in terms of values, generic skills and specific competencies. The draft curriculum framework circulated in Northern Ireland in 1999 secured approval ratings of 90% for its proposed underpinning values.

---

**Proposed value framework for the Northern Ireland curriculum reform process**

*It is proposed that the following values are clearly stated as underpinning each of the curriculum objectives:*
1. *We value each individual's unique capacity for spiritual, moral, emotional, physical and intellectual growth;*
2. *We value equality, justice and human rights within our society and our capacity as citizens to resolve conflict by democratic means;*
3. *We value the environment as the basis of life and the need to sustain it for future generations;*
4. *We value each individual's right to work and to earn a living in accordance with personal preference and attributes (CCEA, 2000; cited in Arlow, 2003).*

---

Internalization of such values by teachers and students, as well as learning to how apply them in real life, is the primary goal of the programmes under discussion in the present study. As will be seen, *the process of internalization requires dedicated time and space in the curriculum, together with committed teachers skilled in nurturing pro-social behaviour change, and supportive structured materials.* All the programmes reviewed here require personal *skills development* by students to enable the translation of the *values* they study into *attitudes and behaviours.*

## MOTIVATIONAL STARTING POINTS, COVERAGE AND NOMENCLATURE

Having touched upon so many overlapping goals, we may now return to the question of nomenclature. As noted earlier, the title given to an education programme aimed at the development or change of social behaviour has to be based on a highly motivating goal, and appropriate for the user and the setting. 'Education for peace' is thus appropriate where there is a deep community commitment to getting out of a situation or cycle of violence or war, as the author observed with refugees from Afghanistan, Sudan and Somalia.[52] It may not be acceptable, however, where there is still a feeling of bitterness, where there is religious commitment to an ongoing 'holy war' or political sensitivity. In this case 'life-skills' might be more acceptable as a title for education in conflict prevention, as was the case for UNHCR's recent initiative in Eritrea. Parents and politicians may not allow 'HIV/AIDS education' or 'reproductive health education' because of religious concerns or the fear of encouraging premarital sex, so 'life-skills' may be an acceptable title for studies that in fact deal with refusal skills for unwanted or unprotected sex.

So far as possible, the title used by teachers and students should carry a *motivational force that will inspire them to make the efforts to teach and learn new behaviours and values.* We are dealing with matters that are of deep concern to people's lives. *'Peace'* is motivational to peoples who have known years of war. *'Human rights'* or *'democracy'* is motivational to people who have been deprived of civic rights and opportunities. *'HIV/AIDS education'* may be motivational to young people in communities severely affected by AIDS. *'Relationship education'* may be motivational to young people in any society.

*Regarding the range of goals to be covered, it is argued in this study that all the goals cited above are relevant to all students worldwide, and that they should all be addressed, as part of a locally constructed unified programme. This programme should give primacy to the titles and concerns with the most motivational force for the student group concerned. Educators should try to co-operate so that this can be achieved.*

What can this unified programme be called? Policy makers and practitioners are hesitant on the one hand to have an umbrella title (such as 'peace education', 'human rights education', 'education for democracy', 'health education', 'life-skills education') that does not mention the name they themselves use. Yet they cannot work with an umbrella title that takes two lines of text each time it is used.[53] There is also the problem that an internationally derived umbrella title may imply inclusion of topics that appear undesirable, inappropriate or politically sensitive in a given country.

*This very real problem of nomenclature should not mean that children are deprived of a good intervention in this area. It may be suggested that educators in a given location should:*

- *Find an umbrella terminology that suits and motivates them;*
- *Check that their proposed educational interventions include all the goals described above, in relevant form;*
- *Check with young people to find titles and content for the programme and its various course units that will motivate them.*

## NOTES

1. The peace researcher Johann Galtung (1969) considered the cessation or absence of violent conflict as 'negative peace', and emphasized that it might not be durable unless 'structural violence' and injustice in society was transformed, to generate 'positive peace'. This distinction has been widely adopted.

2. The term 'pro-social' refers to behaviours supporting the well-being of others, as contrasted to 'anti-social'.

3. Many of these goals are themselves the subject, and highly motivational title, of separate 'educational initiatives'.

4. For a general overview of issues related to education and conflict, see, for example, Tawil, 1997; Retamal & Aedo-Richmond, 1998; Bush & Saltarelli, 2000; WEF, 2000b; Crisp et al., 2001; Smith & Vaux, 2002; Sommers, 2002; Triplehorn, 2002; Isaacs, 2002; Tawil & Harley, 2004; Machel, 1996, 2001; Sinclair, 2001, 2002.

5. The *'Batissons la Paix'* initiative in Burundi in the mid-1990s was well-liked by teachers (personal communication from Anna Obura, then UNICEF Regional Education Adviser). However, *Batissons la Paix* was based on student kits that were relatively expensive (for drawing, colouring, cutting and pasting pictures relating to peace, etc.), which limited sustainability.

6. The success of the Kukatonon (meaning 'We are one') Peace Theatre initiative by the Christian Health Association of Liberia led to an Education Ministry initiative supported by UNICEF to train school personnel in conflict resolution (Fountain, 1997). Liberian refugee educators in neighbouring Guinea revived elements of this programme as an introduction to conflict resolution in the school health education programme of the NGO International Rescue Committee in the mid-1990s.

7. International instruments adopted by the UNESCO General Conference (governments represented by their Education Ministers) include the 1974 *Recommendation concerning Education for International Understanding, Co-operation and Peace and Education relating to Human Rights and Fundamental Freedoms,* and the 1995 *Resolution on Education for Peace, Human Rights, Democracy, International Understanding and Tolerance.* See also good practice collections (such as UNESCO, 1997a, 2003a), guidelines (e.g. Balasooriya, 2001, Weil, 2002) and relevant sections of the UNESCO website (www.unesco.org).

8. Angela Commisso, personal communication; Devadoss, 2000, p. 41-42.

9. See case study 3, Chapter IV.

10. See www.ifor.org. The Center for Non-violent Communication, California, has a skills-based methodology developed in the US by Marshall Rosenberg (1999) and used both for formal and non-formal education in many other countries (see www.cnvc.org). The 1999 'Hague Appeal for Peace' led to an international survey of peace education initiatives (see www.haguepeace.org, www.ipb.org) and a manual drawing on the survey contributions (Reardon & Cabezudo, 2002). See also Miller & Affolter (2002) for a sample of NGO projects. There are many regional or sub-regional initiatives, such as the numerous education programmes seeking to build a constituency for peaceful coexistence between Israelis and Palestinians (see, for

example, Halperin, 1997; Salomon & Nevo, 2002).

11. Nevo & Brem (2002) analysed seventy-nine evaluations of peace education programmes across the world in terms of purpose, age group, didactic approach, and duration. They found, quite cheeringly, that fifty-one were effective, eighteen partially effective and only ten ineffective.

12. Salomon (2002). He suggests that the goals for peace education in regions of intractable conflict should relate to changing the perception of the other side's collective narrative of the conflict, through legitimization of their collective narrative, critical examination of one's own side's contribution to the conflict, empathy, and a disposition for non-violent problem-solving.

13. See www.haguepeace.org. The May 1999 Hague Appeal for Peace Conference, held on the anniversary of the 1899 Hague Peace Conference, led to a Global Campaign for Peace Education.

14. Reardon and Cabezudo (2002: Book 1, p. 19).

15. In the author's view, 'might is right' is unacceptable; but might exists and carries responsibility to help minimize the use of violence. Where action is needed to restrain aggression, the widest range of support from parties known for good faith should be ensured, with actions remaining within the norms of international human rights instruments, humanitarian law and the Charter of the United Nations. Students can be helped to form their own views on these matters from an early age, beginning with examples of how schools and students should respond to bullying.

16. See, for example, Heyneman (1998), Heyneman & Todoric-Bebic (2000), Ritzen & Woolcock (2000).

17. As in a recent World Bank dialogue on education for 'Promoting peace and respect for diversity'.

18. Tawil & Harley (2004) use the term 'identity-based conflict' where others might say 'ethnic conflict', pointing to the need in many societies for a more inclusive national identity, as well as covering situations where there is no clear agreement about the existence of a particular nation State (as has been the case in Bosnia-Herzegovina, Sri Lanka and Northern Ireland).

19. See, for example, Mitchell (2003). The Southern Poverty Law Center in the US has published *'Teaching Tolerance'* magazine since 1992 (see www.teachingtolerance.org,).

20. See, for example, Finkbeiner & Koplin (2002).

21. Maoz (2002), in an evaluation of forty-seven programmes of education for coexistence through inter-group encounters between Jews and Arabs in Israel, distinguished three types of programme: models based on similarity and tolerance (60%), models based on confrontation (13%) and intermediate models based on working through conflict by means such as sharing personal life stories (21%).

22. See, for example, Kennedy & Mellor (2002), Kennedy (undated).

23. For other introductory manuals see, for example, UNESCO (1998), Tibbitts (1997a), Elbers (2000), OHCHR (undated).

24. Felisa Tibbitts (2002) distinguishes three levels of human rights education: level 1 – values and awareness-raising in the general population, working towards a critical mass of societal support; level 2 –'accountability', for professionals whose work

deals with vulnerable groups, the law, etc; and level 3, 'transformational', to empower communities to work towards the prevention of abuses.

25. Even conservative Pushtun elders in Afghan refugee camps in Pakistan, who in the 1980s and early 1990s had refused to let their daughters attend school, now demand access to schooling, so that their daughters may become literate (reports from UNHCR field staff and personal observation).

26. Connell (2000) refers to 'multiple masculinities' and the fact that masculinities are constructed under specific historical circumstances. See also other papers in *Male roles and masculinities: a culture of peace perspective* (Breines et al., 2000).

27. In a recent UNICEF survey of curriculum, thirty-eight of the fifty-four respondent countries stated they had gender-inclusive curriculum strategies in place or under development. Most entailed textbook review, to eliminate gender stereotypes. Some countries reported that gender issues were systematically incorporated in all subjects, while others mentioned their incorporation into life skills, civic and moral education, and language classes. Training of textbook writers and training of teachers to call equally on girls in the classroom were typical interventions (UNICEF, 2000).

28. Reardon (2001, p. 155) defines gender equality as assurance of the equal human worth and dignity of women and men.

29. NGOs can play a major role. Government community workers trained by Swedish Save the Children in Pakistan provided 'gender training' to the male social welfare committees in Afghan refugee camps. Surprisingly, the committee members, conservative Pushtun elders, expressed their appreciation, citing examples such as their new awareness of the health hazards for their wives of carrying water over difficult terrain, stating that older boys and youths were being encouraged to help out (personal observation, 1999).

30. Olweus (1996), Ruiz (1998). The level of bullying varies between schools, with up to 50% of children in some British primary schools reporting having been bullied and 5%-10% of children experiencing persistent bullying over a long period of their school lives (Smith & Stephenson, 1991; Sharp et al., 2002, cited in Oliver & Candappa, 2003). For an overview of violence at school see Ohsako (1997). Salmi (2000) sets education in the context of the heritage of direct, indirect, repressive and alienating violence in society and cites programmes designed to overcome violence and improve respect for human rights.

31. Prevention of bullying is a topic that cannot be treated in full here. Successful anti-bullying programmes require development of a code of conduct in consultation with students, training of teachers and ancillary staff to detect and cope with bullying, explicit lessons on the subject of bullying, involvement of students through class and school councils, and use of 'pupil helpers' or 'peer supporters', trained to listen to and support those involved in bullying. 'Peer mediators' often deal with bullying incidents. Anti-bullying programmes need to be continually refreshed, otherwise bullying may recur (Eslea & Smith, 1994). This finding supports the view that education on behaviour and values needs to be implemented on a continuing and progressive basis throughout the years of schooling. See websites such as that of Educators for Social Responsibility (www.esrnational.org) for further details of

programmes that have reduced bullying and violence in schools in the USA, and www.dfes.gov.uk/bullying/, www.citizenshipfoundation.org.uk, for initiatives and research in the UK; also Thorne (1995, p. 179), Smith & Samara (2003).

32. In the UK, schools have been expected to provide 'personal, social and health education', and there is now a recommendation to focus on the development of 'emotional and social competence' (Weare & Gray, 2003). For a comprehensive guide to skills-based health education, see WHO (2003a, 2003b). See also Peace Corps (2001).

33. This bears directly on girls' right to education. Many studies have shown that families in developing countries withdraw their daughters from school because of other girls becoming pregnant as a result of sexual relationships with fellow students, as well as teacher harassment (making examination results dependent on sexual favours), sugar daddies (who provide clothes and books for school in return for favours) and harassment while in transit to and from school. These factors can be enhanced in situations of emergency and conflict. Teachers and students have to learn how to move away from these patterns of behaviour, especially in the context of the AIDS epidemic.

34. There are many interpretations of the concept of citizenship. For a list of forty-one such concepts, see Keogh (2003, p. 9-10).

35. For an overview of the transition and its implications for the teaching of courses related to citizenship in some East European countries see, for example, Budiene (2001), Valdmaa (2002), Georgescu & Palade (2003).

36. As emphasized by Meyer-Bisch (1995, p. 13-16), students must learn that democracy is an *'extending'* concept (the possibility of more responsibilities and rights) but also a *'limiting'* concept. The wishes of a person, or of the majority in society, must be constrained by respect for the human rights of others. Students should learn that under democracy, parties that win an election should not do just anything they please, but must observe the internationally agreed norms and standards of human rights and the rule of law, as well as promoting the future welfare of citizens through building social cohesion and national unity.

37. The Argentine curriculum indicates that 'relativism' and 'fundamentalism' should be countered by promoting universal values such as promotion of good, the search for truth, life, human dignity, love, peace, living together, solidarity, friendship, mutual understanding justice, freedom, tolerance, honesty, international and intercultural understanding (Cox, 2002, p. 111).

38. Key competencies sought in education for democratic citizenship are identified by the Council of Europe's Recommendation 2002/12 as 'the ability to: settle conflicts in a non-violent manner; argue in defence of one's viewpoint; listen to, understand and interpret other people's arguments; recognize and accept differences; make choices, consider alternatives and subject them to ethical analysis; shoulder shared responsi-bilities; establish constructive, non-aggressive relations with others; and develop a critical approach to information, thought patterns and philosophical, religious, social, political and cultural concepts, at the same time remaining committed to fundamental values and principles of the the Council of Europe.' (COE, 2002)

39. Birzea (2002). See also Spajic-Vrkas (2002), Trajkowski (2002) and other papers from the 'Stocktaking Research Project' on education for democratic citizenship in South East Europe; Smith et al., 2002; see the South-East European Co-operation Network website: www.see-educoop.net

40. As an example from Eastern Europe, the pilot project for citizenship education in secondary schools in Ukraine focuses on rights and duties, stereotypes, conflicts, school/family/peers, crime (grade nine); political institutions and processes, civil society, democracy, elections, mass media (grade ten); market economy, social security, multiculturalism, Ukraine and the world (grade eleven) (Pozniak, 2003, p. 184).

41. Evaluations within the US have shown the positive impact of Project Citizen on civic knowledge, skills and participation. Likewise, an evaluation in 1999 of 2000 Bosnian students, half of whom had participated in Project Citizen, showed that participating students' political knowledge, skills and tolerance were significantly higher than those of control students. Similar results were found in Latvia and Lithuania (Soule, 2001). Environmental education, an important part of modern citizenship, should likewise have an action base. In schools, this may refer more to awareness-raising role-plays and community-service activities, such as tree-planting and environmental sanitation, while at adult level, NGOs can create links to remedial action (Dillon et al., 2001).

42. The Civic Culture Programme in Bogota, 1995-97, illustrates a multi-sectoral civic education initiative, which led to measurable results. It was supported by an exemplary survey of attitudes to 'civic coexistence' among 1,400 grade nine students, which interestingly showed that 'the two main factors in co-existence proved to be the capacity to draw up and comply with agreements and to respect the law, [...] a better predictor of the absence of violence inflicted by youngster on youngster' (Mockus, 2002, p. 30). The survey indicated that the law needed to be backed by cultural endorsement to be effective, and the subsequent Civic Culture Programme, 2001-03, emphasized democratic culture as a means of increasing cultural support for the rule of law.

43. Case study presented by John Rutayisire at UNESCO International Bureau of Education Colloquium on *Curriculum Change and Social Cohesion in Conflict-affected Societies,* Geneva, April 2003.

44. See, for example, McKeown (undated); UNESCO (2002a). For the interrelationship between multicultural and environmental education, see Gagliardi & Mosconi (1995).

45. The present study does not attempt an overview of environmental education. However, environmental issues will feature strongly in role-plays, service activities, etc., in education for peace, citizenship, gender equity, etc. It is recommended that behavioural skills and values promoting concern for ecological sustainability and environmental sanitation feature as special modules in the integrated approach to education for living together suggested in Chapters V and VI below.

46. The other key themes are: overcoming poverty, health promotion, water, rural transformation, sustainable consumption, sustainable tourism, indigenous knowledge, media and communication technologies, as well as environmental protection and sustainability (www.unesco.org).

47. Many other types of programmes could be cited besides those discussed above,

including 'character education', moral education, ethics, etc. (Titus, 1994).

48. Puig (1995) refers to private or micro-ethical (personal) and public or macro-ethical (instrumental) values (cited in Garcia & Barriga, 2002).

49. For a values framework for early childhood, see UNESCO (2002c).

50. Birzea (1996) noted that in post-communist Eastern Europe, key values for education included strengthening of citizenship, universal values, national identity, rediscovery of religion and of the European ideal; and that most countries were introducing a variant of citizenship education as a separate subject at secondary and sometimes primary level, mostly taught by social science teachers.

51. For a discussion of values implicit in conventional school subjects, and in the 'cross-cutting' area of education for mutual understanding in Northern Ireland, see Smith & Montgomery (1997).

52. Aguilar & Retamal (1998, p. 33) stress that emergency education for conflict-affected populations should include 'survival' themes, including mine-awareness education, health awareness, environmental awareness, and education for peace and reconciliation, drawing on their own perceptions of the situation that confronts them. 'The research and assessment of these "generative themes" are an important part of the dialogue between the educators and the populations affected by the humanitarian crisis. These contents constitute the foundation for building a basic safety net of knowledge and understanding for these populations... [and] are [Freire's] concrete "hinges" for opening the door towards a more complex reflection about peace and reconciliation.'

53. Educators should avoid arguments such as 'peace education is the most wide-ranging concept and includes human rights as one component'; 'human rights education is the all-encompassing concept and includes education for peace, conflict resolution and citizenship'; 'citizenship education is the best title and includes human rights, peace and conflict resolution'; 'life-skills education does/does not include the skills for peace, conflict resolution and human rights'; 'gender education should be a separate topic/should be integrated in other topics'; etc.

CHAPTER III

# Internalizing skills, values and behaviours

Education in its usual form does not automatically bring about peace, democracy or respect for the rights and well-being of others, as the history of the twentieth century shows all too clearly. Special efforts are needed if education is to promote such goals (Smith & Vaux, 2002). The remainder of this study attempts to identify the efforts required in the curriculum field.

A first step is to look at what educational theory can tell us about building concepts, skills, attitudes and values that are supportive of peace, tolerance, human rights, active citizenship and healthy living. We examine various theories including Bloom's taxonomy of cognitive and affective learning, 'social cognitive learning', 'social and emotional learning', and the stages of child development. These paradigms have been used in designing programmes of the type considered in the present study. The review of theory will support this book's thesis, that well-planned and repeated participative educational activities focused on skills and values are needed, if the goals in Chapter II are to be attained.[1] We shall find that special measures will be required: *special clearly identified study time and special teacher training and support for special experiential learning activities to build specific and clearly understood skills and values.*

## DEVELOPING HIGHER LEVEL COGNITIVE SKILLS

Bloom's influential *Taxonomy of educational objectives* (1964) put forward a hierarchy of cognitive educational objectives, together with hierarchies of objectives for the affective and psycho-motor domains. The aim was to broaden educators' thinking about educational objectives, which often remain on the 'lower' levels of cognitive learning, notably *knowledge acquisition and recall, comprehension and 'application'*. The relative ease of assessing these levels of learning means that they feature strongly in examinations, and that teachers, parents and students often see them as the essence of schooling.

In contrast, all the programmes considered in the present study rely heavily on the higher levels of cognitive learning, which are identified in Bloom's Taxonomy as *analysis, synthesis, and evaluation*. Practising the use of higher level skills in relation to a particular topic in the school curriculum often takes the form of essays, reflection, small group and class activities and discussion, debates, and in some subject areas, role plays, dramas and artistic presentations. These activities are time-consuming. With an overcrowded timetable and examination pressures, the higher-level objectives are thus often under-represented due to lack of time. They also represent a challenge to teachers, especially if the latter are not familiar with such methods or lack mastery and self-confidence with respect to the subject area or activity concerned. Moreover, these higher level skills, practised occasionally and in an unco-ordinated way across different subjects, are often not introduced to students by name. Without reflecting on the nature of these higher-order cognitive processes, it is difficult for students to build up skills in them.

For this reason, programmes such as education for peace, citizenship, human rights and HIV/AIDS avoidance often have to introduce the higher-level cognitive skills as such, to ensure that students become aware of them and know how to use them, before moving on to apply them to the theme of the particular course. For example, the cognitive skill of *creative problem-solving* (using Bloom's *analysis, synthesis, and evaluation*) may be introduced by means of puzzles, mathematical challenges and games. How many triangles can be counted in a large triangle containing many smaller ones? How many games of football are needed to complete a tournament? How can the beautiful but poor girl avoid having to marry the cruel moneylender? How can the wolf, goat and cabbage all be ferried across the river in stages to avoid the cabbage or goat being eaten? These examples from the peace education programme developed by UNHCR serve to introduce problem-solving as an intellectual activity, requiring calm consideration, divergent thinking, avoiding unwarranted assumptions, visualization of the problem, co-operative group work, and sometimes envisaging the possibility of multiple win-win solutions. The programme in fact uses these abstract examples as an introduction to certain aspects of conflict prevention or resolution, with class discussion on issues such as the way assumptions can lead to misunderstandings that may lead to conflict. The programme then applies problem-solving skills to negotiation and conflict-resolution activities.

Some educators regard the improvement of teaching methodology, notably more use of high-level cognitive skills and 'constructivist' child-centred approaches, as the best way to prepare students to face the challenges in their personal lives and societies. The International Reading Association's *Reading and writing for critical thinking* programme (described in Chapter IV below) focuses on pedagogical improvements of this kind as the key to education for democracy, on the basis that students who learn critical thinking and practise debate in the classroom will be better equipped for democratic citizenship.

Most of the programmes discussed here incorporate the application of higher-level cognitive skills to the specifics of the social issues motivating the programme. This helps the *transfer of competence* in the skills to their applications in promoting peace, resisting peer pressure, active citizenship, etc. The skills are *practised or rehearsed in relation to the particular goal,* as when students analyse a problem they have recently been part of, or act out role-plays based on a dispute in their community. The 'six-step' approach for solving disputes may be introduced, for example.

---

Six-step problem-solving for conflict resolution: application of the cognitive skills of analysis, creative thinking and synthesis

- What does each side want?
- What is the problem?
- How many solutions can be found?
- Which solutions are acceptable?
- What is the best solution, benefiting both sides?
- Was the problem solved or did it re-surface? [2]

---

In the 'life-skills' literature, the higher-level cognitive skills are often presented in relation to decision-making and problem-solving regarding health issues. Gillespie (2002) includes in 'life-skills' education for HIV/AIDS education the use of cognitive skills to analyse prevalent cultural norms and the consequences of different lines of action:

---

**Decision-making/problem-solving skills**
- Information gathering skills
- Evaluating future consequences of present actions for self and others
- Determining alternative solutions to problems
- Analysis skills regarding the influence of values and attitudes of self and others on motivation

**Critical thinking skills**
- Analysing peer and media influences
- Analysing attitudes, values, social norms and beliefs and factors affecting these
- Identifying relevant information and information sources.

---

## DEVELOPING AFFECTIVE OR VALUING SKILLS
## AND BEHAVIOUR PATTERNS

Building skills in the cognitive domain alone does not suffice for pro-social behavioural skills and values development, although it provides useful tools. Indeed, cognitive skills can be and are used to plan self-serving or anti-social activities. Clearly, we must also consider the realm of attitudes and values — Bloom's affective domain. His affective educational objectives are rather awkwardly named, perhaps because the English language has not been adequately developed in that dimension. The lower level objectives begin with 'receiving phenomena' and then 'responding to phenomena', which basically refer to paying careful attention to an event, idea or information. The higher level affective objectives move from 'valuing' to 'organizing of values' and then to 'internalizing values'.[3] This corresponds in a general way to the 'values clarification' model of 'prizing' one's beliefs and behaviours, choosing one's beliefs and behaviours, and acting on one's beliefs.[4]

A special pedagogy is needed to involve and impact on the personal identity of the students, so they not only notice that the teacher is saying that prejudice is a bad thing, for example, but actually feel it. This requires the interaction of the cognitive and affective domains. The pedagogy can be fairly conventional at times, as when students listen to parts of a story and then discuss as a class what they would do in that situation or what they feel is the right thing to do. A more active pedagogy is also needed, where students explore their own and their peers' feelings and competencies as they undertake some 'stimulus activity' as individuals or in pairs or small groups, such as communication and perception exercises, co-operative activities, role-plays or practising assertiveness, refusal or mediation skills. Participative discussion, within a values context of concern for others, helps students internalize their learnings at the end of the lesson.

FIGURE 1: **The Bloom hierarchy of affective and cognitive education objectives** [5]

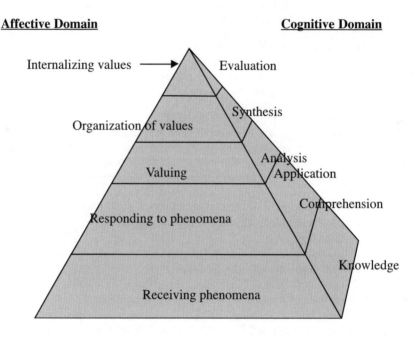

**Affective Domain**     **Cognitive Domain**

The cognitive and affective domains must both be taken into account in the design and implementation of education for peace, human rights, citizenship and 'life-skills' programmes. Effective communication, for example, is a basic feature of many such programmes, and has an affective as well as a cognitive component. The key skill of 'active listening', when used as a tool for conflict prevention and mediation, requires listening respectfully to the speaker as a person communicating something as he or she perceives it, and controlling one's emotions, as one may not agree with the speaker or may be facing someone who is on the 'other side' of a conflict. It also entails providing tactful feedback to ensure the accuracy of what one has heard and facilitate communication. In the Bloom taxonomy, 'active listening' might come under the 'comprehension' and 'analysis' aspects of the cognitive dimension, and under the 'receiving phenomena' and 'responding to phenomena' aspects of the affective domain. Active listening is a fundamental tool of education for the goals in Chapter II, and is incorporated in many programmes. It needs to be practised as a skill through role plays, and *these take time.*

---

**Role plays of poor listening and active listening**

1. Trainer first demonstrates poor listening skills while volunteer attempts to make a request or narrate an event (trainer yawns exaggeratedly, is distracted, shuffles papers, interrupts the speaker to do other things, looks out of the window and does not make eye contact — this can be very funny if well acted).
2. Trainer asks group what was wrong with this method of communication.
3. Trainer models good active listening skills (affective skills: trainer has friendly and attentive manner, makes eye contact, has good body language; cognitive skills: trainer clarifies information, asks questions, gives summaries of information received and feelings experienced by speaker, asks for feedback).
4. Trainer asks group what was right about this method of communication.
5. Trainees practise active listening in groups of three, taking turns as speaker, listener and observer.[6]

---

The more advanced skill of mediation requires a good balance of cognitive and affective skills and values. Practice is needed *and takes time*.

---

**Cognitive-affective profile for effective mediator**[7]

- Believes and feels we are all more similar than we are different.
- Active listener, with an open heart, trying to understand how the other person feels.
- Communicates effectively, saying what is meant and not speaking from anger or fear.
- Believes in co-operation, in working together to find solutions, even if not liking the person concerned.
- Recognizes own emotions, not allowing them to negatively affect behaviour.
- Recognizes that everyone has a point of view and the right to express it.
- Understands that there are often many ways of solving problems, and that it is 'win-win' solutions that last.

---

The cognitive and affective elements of Bloom's framework are clearly very relevant to the design of education for peace, human rights, active citizenship and preventive health. However, the systematic application of the taxonomy in the design of an education programme could be very complex. In practice, the educator often designs a programme from a general understanding of Bloom's principles combined with experience of 'what works'. Nevertheless, the taxonomy can help in clarifying the rationale for skills- and values-based programmes, in improving programme design and for purposes of evaluation.[8, 9]

## SOCIAL COGNITIVE LEARNING

Another paradigm that has been influential in the design of education for behavioural development and change is social cognitive learning theory, developed by Albert Bandura and others.[10] Social cognitive learning brings in the psychological dimension, with an emphasis on self-regulation and goal setting, self-reflection and feelings of self-efficacy. The theory incorporates 'vicarious' learning — learning through observing other people's behaviours and their consequences. It suggests repeated practice of desired behaviours through simulated situations in which learners are not afraid to make mistakes, namely multiple role plays leading to feelings of self-efficacy with regard to new behaviours.

This theory has been extensively applied in the field of preventive health, in programmes to provide children with skills for coping with internal aspects of their social lives, including stress reduction, self-control and decision-making. Another implication of the theory is the importance of using the natural processes by which children learn behaviour, including observation, role-play and peer education as well as plain instruction (Mangrulkar et al., 2001).

Although applied mostly in the field of health, social cognitive learning theory is relevant likewise to areas of behavioural skills, values and attitudinal development, such as education for active citizenship, respect for human rights and conflict management. Educators interested in these fields must take note of research studies such as the review by Kirby et al (1994)[11] that showed that more effective school-based programmes for HIV/AIDS prevention followed the principles of social cognitive theory. More successful programmes were experiential and focused clearly on the desired behavioural outcomes. These:

- were based on social cognitive or other cognitive behavioural theory;
- used clear statements regarding the consequences of unprotected intercourse and how to avoid them (through delayed intercourse or condom use);
- rewarded values implying disapproval of unprotected intercourse;
- highlighted the role of social influence in sexual decision-making;
- used interactive, observational and rehearsal strategies to develop communication and negotiation skills and to personalize the risks;
- involved small-group practice or more than fourteen hours contact time;
- provided quality training for those delivering the intervention.

Another study identified 'four fundamental intervention activities' associated with behaviour change for effective HIV/AIDS prevention, which are in line with social cognitive theory:[12]

**Instruction:** providing an explanation and rationale for learning the new skill

**Modeling:** providing an example of effective enactment of the behaviour provided by a credible model

**Practice:** role-playing potential risk-inducing situations to practise the new behaviour
**Feedback:** using feedback on performance from group leader and fellow group members to support and reinforce behaviour changes.

The related health education theory of social influence and 'psychological inoculation' carries the important message that children should be taught about particular behaviours before they reach the age when peers will pressure them, for example, to smoke, take drugs, or have premature and unprotected sex. 'Teaching children resistance skills is more effective at reducing problem behaviours than just providing information or provoking fear of the results of the behaviour' (Whitman & Aldinger, 2002).[13]

Social learning theory thus validates the idea of starting skills-based programmes for peace, citizenship, human rights and preventive health at a young age. It also shows the importance of moving from generic skills development to their application in specific contexts, whether in avoiding conflicts in the queue for water, resisting bullying or supporting community projects as active citizens.[14]

## DISSONANCE THEORY AND THE 'FEET-FIRST' APPROACH

Dissonance theory likewise supports the need for practising new behaviours repeatedly, in safe situations. Dissonance research shows that when people act in a way inconsistent with their previous attitudes and values, they tend to change their beliefs to rationalize and justify their new behaviours. Thus, signing a petition for a cause or purchase of a pin supporting the cause tends to increase a person's donation to that cause at a later date. McCauley (2002) relates this to the problem of linking participation in a 'diversity training' workshop including members of different ethnic groups to subsequent behaviours. He suggests that practising specific 'real world' cross-ethnic behaviours in the safe space of the workshop can be a small step facilitating these behaviours later.[15] Dissonance theory thus reinforces the message of this study that the development and change of behaviour-related skills and values require special measures, with a great deal of personal involvement through role-plays, rehearsal of specific actions and skills, etc., which means special time.

Pro-social or citizenship behaviours can be practised from an early age 'feet first' through arrangements for service in the school or community, thus creating a habit of positive pro-social behaviours.

## TESTIMONY AND BONDING

Peer group support (the converse of dissonance) is important in moving towards values such as reconciliation, active citizenship, respect for human rights and

> **Promote community service to build empathy**
>
> *Community service plays an essential role in fostering generalization of social-emotional skills, particularly in building empathy.*
> *-Properly conducted community service, which begins at the earliest level of schooling and continues through all subsequent years, provides an opportunity for children to learn life-skills, integrate them, apply them, reflect upon them and then demonstrate them [and] broaden their sense of perspective and build empathic understanding and caring connections to the world around them (Elias, 2003, p. 17).*

resistance to pressure for risky behaviours. The creation within the classroom and timetable of a special space and time for personal testimony and exchange of views on these behavioural and value-rich issues with significant others can reinforce resolve, if we extrapolate from the extensive use of group discussions for all kinds of therapy, from Alcoholics Anonymous to Weight-Watchers.[16]

Where the programme incorporates testimony of personal histories in encounters between conflicting parties, there can be a broadening of the sense of identity from that of being a 'victim', together with the formation of friendships across groups, and in some instances a greater acceptance of the other group's 'collective narrative' (Salomon, 2003).

## DEVELOPING PERSON-BASED COMPETENCIES AND VALUES

Educators concerned with helping young people confront life problems and challenges have put these and other theories together to develop schemas of educational objectives based on the perceived competencies required. These schemas include cognitive, affective, social and psychological dimensions.[17]

For example, the Collaborative to Advance Social and Emotional Learning (CASEL) in the USA has developed a research-based framework to help schools enhance their students' health and reduce the prevalence of problem behaviours such as drug use, violence and high-risk sexual activities (Payton et al. 2000; Elias, 2003). The framework includes a values dimension, *positive attitudes and values;* and three cognitive/values/psychological complexes, *responsible decision-making, awareness of self and others, and social interaction skills*. This model was built originally around the dilemma of an American student facing difficult choices when lacking self-esteem, subject to peer pressure and/or confused about his or her own emotions and best interests.[18] However, many of the educational objectives set out in the CASEL framework are highly relevant to the wider goals of Chapter II.

**CASEL model of social and emotional learning competencies needed by students**

*Awareness of self and others*
*Awareness of feelings:* can accurately perceive and label one's feelings
- **Management of feelings:** can regulate one's feelings
- **Constructive sense of self:** can accurately perceive one's strengths and weaknesses and handle everyday challenges with confidence and optimism
- **Perspective-taking:** can accurately perceive the perspectives of others.

*Positive attitudes and values*
- **Personal responsibility:** intention to engage in safe and healthy behaviours and be honest and fair in dealing with others
- **Respect for others:** intention to accept and appreciate individual and group differences and to value the rights of all people
- **Social responsibility:** intention to contribute to the community and protect the environment.

*Responsible decision-making*
- **Problem identification:** can identify situations that require a decision and assess the risks, barriers and resources
- **Social norm analysis:** can critically evaluate social, cultural and media messages pertaining to social norms and personal behaviour
- **Adaptive goal- setting:** can set positive and realistic goals
- **Problem-solving:** can develop, implement and evaluate positive and informed solutions to problems.

*Social interaction skills*
- **Active listening:** can attend to others both verbally and non-verbally to show that they have been understood
- **Expressive communication:** can initiate and maintain conversations and express thoughts and feelings verbally and non-verbally
- **Co-operation:** can take turns and share in pairs and group situations
- **Negotiation:** can consider all perspectives involved in a conflict in order to resolve it peacefully and to the satisfaction of all involved
- **Refusal:** can make and follow through with clear 'No' statements, to avoid pressure and delay acting in pressured situations until prepared.
- **Help-seeking:** can identify the need for support and assistance and access available and appropriate resources (Payton et al., 2000, p.6).

There are many similar schemas, which essentially contain similar elements arranged in different combinations.[19] The model adopted reflects the problems foremost in the educator's mind. For example, the model developed by Amaya Gillespie of UNICEF reflects the organization's concern with the tragedy of the AIDS epidemic affecting so many young people in Africa and elsewhere. The goal here is for young people to reconsider cultural traditions that help spread the disease, especially (in many cultures) through education empowering girls to say 'No' to unwanted or unprotected sex and enabling boys to understand the harmful consequences to themselves and others of a casual approach to sex.[20] The 'decision-making and critical thinking' part of her schema was cited earlier. She also identifies the objectives of 'communication and inter-personal skills', 'coping and self-management skills', and skills for managing feelings and stress that comprise complexes of cognitive, affective/values and psychological dimensions:

---

**Communication and inter-personal skills**
- **Inter-personal communication skills:** verbal/non-verbal communication; active listening; expressing feelings (giving feedback without blaming)
- **Negotiation/refusal skills:** negotiation and conflict management; assertiveness skills; refusal skills
- **Empathy:** ability to listen and understand another's needs and circumstances and express that understanding[21]
- **Co-operation and teamwork:** expressing respect for others' contributions and different styles; assessing one's own abilities and contributing to the group
- **Advocacy skills.**

**Coping and self-management skills**
- Skills for increasing internal locus of control
- Self-esteem/confidence-building skills
- Self-awareness skills, including awareness of rights, influences, values, attitudes, strengths and weaknesses.

**Skills for managing feelings**
- Anger management
- Dealing with grief and anxiety
- Coping skills for dealing with loss, abuse and trauma.

**Skills for managing stress**
- Time management
- Positive thinking
- Relaxation techniques (Gillespie, 2002).

---

Clearly the competencies and values in these schemas, which were developed from the viewpoint of 'skills-based' health education or 'life-skills', are very relevant also to programmes focusing on learning to live together: education for peace, responsible citizenship and respect for human rights.

## EFFECTS OF TRAUMA

Students who have been exposed to major trauma may have special social and emotional needs. Educators regularly face children who have suffered bereavement or live with difficult home situations, and who need help with coping skills. The issue of 'psycho-social' needs has come to the fore, however, in the field of education in emergencies, where large numbers of children may have been exposed to armed conflict or massacres, or displaced as refugees away from their extended families and friends. As noted by Macksoud (1993) and Gupta (2000), children react to such stressful experiences in different ways, with very young children not understanding much but feeling insecure, school-age children using fantasy, feeling guilt and restlessness, and perhaps regressing to infantile behaviour, and adolescents becoming anxious, withdrawn or aggressive.

One concern is to strengthen the characteristics that have been identified with 'resilience' in children, including communication and problem-solving skills, self-esteem and self-control (internal protective factors), and an educational climate that is open and supportive, as well as other external protective factors (McCallin, 1996; Nicolai, 2003; Nicolai and Triplehorn, 2003; IRC, 2003). Educators and social workers have stressed the need for structured play and other expressive and physical activities in early emergency (ISCA, 1996; Tolfree, 1996; Aguilar & Retamal, 1998; Retamal, 2000; Sinclair, 2001; Aguilar, 2003). The activity-based approach to education for peace or social and emotional 'life-skills' described in the present study would appear to meet the criteria for reinforcing resilience.[22] However, there is a need to build bridges between the specialists dealing with psycho-social trauma and those dealing with education for peace, citizenship, human rights, and preventive health — to look more closely at commonalities and special approaches needed to meet psycho-social needs in post-emergency conditions and for severely affected children.

## ROLE OF TEXTBOOKS AND TEACH/LEARNING MATERIALS

Textbooks are one of the most important tools for effective education in normal school subjects.[23] Education authorities should therefore consider whether their textbooks support the goals discussed in Chapter II. There has long been concern that textbooks glamourize war, extol the glories of students' own nations and encourage prejudice against others. Exercises in international textbook revision began after the First World War, and were supported by the League of Nations. The Member States of UNESCO adopted a resolution on adapting textbooks to promote international understanding at the organization's first General Conference of Education Ministers in 1946.

The focus has been mainly on history, geography and civics textbooks. Institutions such as the Georg Eckert Institute have promoted bilateral commissions whereby historians from countries that have previously been enemies work together to adjust their respective history textbooks to promote better relations in the future.[24] History teaching now includes elements relevant to understanding of others, through the use of multiple perspectives and multiple sources for teaching about a particular event or situation, through encouraging empathy with people from the past as well as critical thinking. However, many of the skills and values discussed in the present study do not figure prominently in the typical process of textbook revision. Design and assessment criteria for reform of textbooks should include a review of their potential contribution to the goals discussed in Chapter II, and of the possibilities for suggesting participative and experiential activities of the type just discussed, through notes at the end of chapters and in teachers' guides.

There is already a practice of auditing schoolbooks for gender bias, whether in the text or the illustrations. The same auditing should be conducted for textbooks in all subjects, regarding their implications for peace, human rights, active citizenship and healthy relationships and behaviours. Moreover, curriculum and textbook specialists should work to ensure that the content of textbooks is chosen so as to give *positive modeling* of peace-making at personal, community and national level, responsible relationships and civic behaviours, care for the environment, and so on. This can be done through stories (factual or fictional) in school 'readers' for language studies, as well as through factual stories included in textbooks of science, social science, mathematics, etc. As we have seen above, vicarious learning through observing new behaviours and their consequences is an important element in 'social cognitive learning' for young people. Reading and discussion of stories is a possible vehicle for this. Since textbook revision takes time, positive modeling can begin through the use of supplementary reading materials, commissioned as part of an initiative to promote learning to live together.

## DEVELOPMENTAL STAGES AND THE CYCLIC CURRICULUM

When designing a school programme for skills and values development in pursuit of the goals in Chapter II, the stages of child development must be considered. For example, the in-service teacher training developed by UNHCR for its peace education programme includes the study of child development, such as: the gradual progress from the young child's egocentrism to interaction, objectivity and perhaps Jung's intrinsic actualization; cognitive development, moving on from the 'concrete activities' for younger children towards the higher levels of the Bloom taxonomy; Kohlberg's theory of moral development, moving through 'pre-conventional' to 'conventional' and 'post-conventional' stages [25]; and Maslow's and Staub's hierarchies of human needs, moving from basic needs/security to belonging, self-esteem and self-actualization (Maslow) or to effectiveness, positive identity, positive connection and comprehension of reality (Staub). [26] In terms of programme design, these principles mean that cognitive activities and reflection on associated attitudes and values in the lower primary school have different objectives from those in higher grades or for adults.

The peace education curriculum for schools developed by Pamela Baxter incorporates these concepts of child development and illustrates their application in the spiral or cyclic curriculum approach. [27] This enables skills, values and concepts to be revisited each year, but with increased depth and sophistication based on the greater maturity and increased life experience of the students.

> Concept development in any field requires the acquisition of masses of data or experiences. The concept is developed by the data being grouped and categorized into a series of ideas. These ideas are also (over time) categorized together to form generalizations (or sub-concepts). Abstract concepts such as peace and justice require a structured acquisition of data, ideas, sub-concepts, themselves abstract. [28]

High-level concepts such as peace, citizenship, human rights and preventive health should be developed not as mere knowledge but as complexes including the cognitive, affective/values, social and psychological dimensions. They should be built from ideas and sub-concepts also including these multiple dimensions, such as active listening, empathy, negotiation, inclusiveness, non-discrimination and personal responsibility.

FIGURE 2: **Formation of a high level concept** [29]

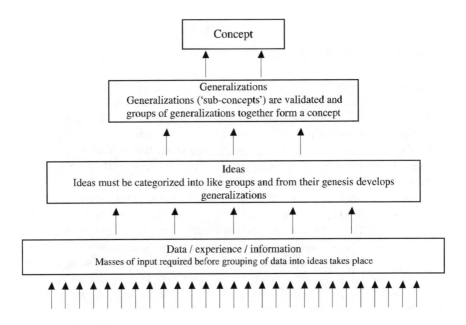

The cyclic curriculum enables children to:

> collect experiences, practise skills, make links and build frameworks within which to practise. In peace education programmes, children need the opportunity to practise the elements of peace, as well as to have positive role models and a safe atmosphere in which to conduct these activities. In the cyclic curriculum the same topic may be taught year after year, but using different data input to help the child build the concept.[30]

It is important to *label* the activities, ideas and concepts in the cyclic curriculum so that the students are fully aware that they are not just discussing a story, having a debate, playing a game of passing a message round the circle or doing a jigsaw together, but are learning skills and developing or deepening ideas relevant to peace, human rights, citizenship or how to live in harmony with their peers. This requires extensive debriefing whereby students discuss together, at a level appropriate to their age, the importance of the skills and values being considered and begin to develop, enrich and internalize a positive idea, behavioural skill or concept. Elias (2003, p. 9) stresses that 'Life-skills that promote academic and social-emotional learning must be taught *explicitly* in every grade level' (emphasis added).

## USING AN ELICITIVE APPROACH

The goals and programmes under discussion here have relevance for many different situations and countries, but only if there is what John Paul Lederach calls an 'elicitive' approach, rather than a 'prescriptive' training model. If a sketch about mediation is written word for word in New York it is likely to miss the mark in Central Africa or Afghanistan. But a role-play about mediation generated by the participants in either location will automatically feature their own settings and concerns. Likewise, the reflection and discussion following an exercise in communication or assertiveness will reflect pro-social behaviour in participants' own environment and culture, if the teacher is from the community concerned. Lederach stresses that the teacher has to be a catalyst and facilitator: 'The participants and their knowledge are seen as the primary resource for the training' drawing on the 'focused experience (theory, practice, multiple setting experience)' of the trainer and the 'implicit knowledge about ways of being/doing in the setting' of the participants (Lederach, 1994, p. 56-57).[31]

The elicitive approach ensures that key issues emerge through group-generated role-plays, etc., regardless of the exact title of the course. For example, an NGO 'peace education' programme for youth in Cambodia includes various health-related and other social issues.

---

**Peace education in Cambodia**

Youth for Peace developed its own curriculum, and its workshops cover the following themes: culture of peace, prejudice and tolerance, national identity, non-violence, human rights, loyalty and good management, and community conflict management [...]. The curriculum is culturally specific, developed by Cambodians for Cambodians, and addresses issues directly relevant to the youth, those being **drugs, HIV/AIDS, trafficking and youth violence.** (Archie, 2003; emphasis added)

---

## THEORY INTO PRACTICE

Enough has been said here to indicate the complexities of designing and implementing education oriented to the goals of peace, respect for human rights, active citizenship, preventive health and so on. The 'hierarchies' of cognitive and affective objectives imply that lower-level skills have to be combined in various ways to create the skills higher in the hierarchy. Affective or values-oriented and attitudinal dimensions have to be combined with cognitive ones. And the psychological dimension is critical in the fusion of these learnings with personal identity — taking 'ownership' of them. The next step in our analysis is therefore to see how practitioners have tackled the challenge of working with these hierarchies and dimensions. Chapter IV will review the content and methodology of specific programmes, noting the teaching/learning models used and their effectiveness.

NOTES

1. This chapter does not attempt a comprehensive review of theories relevant to the learning of the skills, values and behaviours involved in learning to live together, but introduces some elements that have been used in relation to the programmes considered here. A more comprehensive but reader-friendly review would be helpful to practitioners.

2. From Lesson 24, Grade 7 of the INEE/UNHCR Peace Education Teachers' Guide, adapted from Fountain (1997).

3. For convenience, the present study mostly uses the term 'values' to cover the affective domain and 'attitudes', and the terms are used interchangeably.

4. Raths et al. (1966), cited in UNESCO (2002b). The seven components in this values clarification model are prizing and cherishing; publicly affirming when appropriate; choosing from alternatives; choosing after consideration of alternatives; choosing freely; acting; acting with a pattern, consistency and repetition. See also Simon et al. (1972) for values clarification exercises (voting, ranking, forced choices, etc., cited in UNESCO, 2002b).

5. As depicted by Pamela Baxter (personal communication).

6. Adapted from INEE/UNHCR Peace Education Programme Community Workshop Manual (INEE, 2002).

7. Adapted from Lesson 27, Grade 8 of the INEE/UNHCR peace education programme for schools (INEE, 2002).

8. Matthew Lipman has explored this relationship through his Philosophy for Children 'novels' and methodology, and especially, during the last decade, through his addition of values-based 'caring thinking' as a higher-order category of thinking alongside 'critical thinking' and 'creative thinking' (Lipman, 1995, 2003; Brunt, 1996; Olsholt, 2001).

9. For a set of values-education activities for teacher trainees or secondary students, based on a cognitive/affective sequential model of knowing, understanding, valuing and acting, see UNESCO (2002b).

10. See, for example, Bandura (1986, 1989) cited in Vilaca and Sequeira (undated). For the gender dimension of inter-personal skills development in the classroom, see Allard & Wilson (1995).

11. Widely cited, e.g. in UNAIDS (1997), King (1999), Schaalma et al. (2002).

12. The study reviewed nineteen random controlled trials of HIV/AIDS education programmes designed to induce sexual behaviour change (Kalichman & Hospers, 1997).

13. The programmes are targeted at very specific risks, linking classroom exercises on resistance to peer pressure to skills for resisting a risk behaviour (e.g. drug use), forming attitudes (e.g. that drug use is wrong or unsafe) and knowledge (harmful health consequences) (Mangrulkar et al., 2001).

14. Likewise, the health education 'theory of reasoned action' and the 'health-belief model' show the influence of perceived beliefs about what others think the person should do (Whitman & Aldinger, 2002). Such theories indicate the importance of learning to analyse social factors influencing one's behaviour, as well as skills for assertiveness and resistance in relation to social pressures, whether for the purposes of health, or of resisting the call to violence or persecution of dis-empowered social groups or individuals.

15. The 'contact hypothesis' that being or working together leads hostile groups to reconcile is not discussed in the present study, which focuses more on curriculum. Research has shown that for inter-group contact to be effective as a tool for peace and mutual respect there must be equal status between the groups, sustained interaction, interdependence in carrying out a common task, support from authorities and potential for the development of friendships (Pettigrew, 1998), conditions that can be difficult to fulfil. McCauley (2002) summarizes this research and points out that inter-group conflict may arise not only from ignorance about the 'out-group' but from devotion to the 'in-group' – the latter being the principal motivation for many soldiers to fight in battle. Devotion to the in-group makes it difficult for an individual to change his or her behaviour on return from a diversity training or HIV/AIDS prevention session, unless others in the group have also participated.

16. Studies of religious-conversion testimony find that the new experience leads to a new view of converts' previous lives, and that their new views are reinforced by giving testimony before others in the group. 'Research indicates that what people profess before a group consolidates belief. Through a subtle interplay between speaker and audience, people come to believe (more strongly) what they (themselves) say' (Rambo, 1993, cited in Fox, 2003, p. 200-201).

17. The social and psychological dimensions cover some of the competencies described as 'emotional intelligence' (see Goleman, 1995; Gardner, 2000). Garcia & Barriga (2002) cite Puig (1995) regarding the role of feelings and emotions in moral behaviour, with 'affective components as a driving force of the conscious processes of reflection and moral action and of the efforts to build a complex moral identity.'

18. For a summary of research supporting the effectiveness of life-skills approaches to preventive health education (reducing delinquent behaviour, inter-personal violence, criminal behaviour, substance abuse, high-risk sexual activity, peer rejection and bullying, anger control, social adjustment and emotional disorders), see Whitman & Aldinger (2002).

19. For example, the schema developed by the World Health Organization for 'life-skills education' or 'psycho-social competence' comprises: decision-making/problem-solving; creative thinking/critical thinking; communication/inter-personal relationships; self-awareness/empathy; coping with emotions/coping with stress (WHO, 1997).

20. They should also practise tactful ways of saying 'No' to injections and other medical treatments where they have reason to doubt that the equipment has been sterilized.

21. The definition of empathy and the extent to which it is a skill, or skill/value/psychological complex that can be learned or strengthened is a topic too complex to discuss in detail here. Some definitions are based on *understanding* other people's feelings. Other definitions include *sharing* those feelings, as in the definition of empathy by Mangrulkar et al. (2001, p. 42) as 'the capacity to share an emotional response with another person, as well as the ability to discriminate the other's perspective and role'.

22. In early emergency, the more straightforward 'games' found in programmes of education for peace, co-operation, etc., can be 'played' without the element of reflection, if the children are not ready or the teachers not yet trained for classroom discussions on these issues (Pamela Baxter, personal communication). Teachers need training in how to include all students in class activities and motivate them with enjoyable activities, to structure lessons clearly in sub-units to help students with concentration problems, and to recognize students who need specialist help (IRC, 2003; Triplehorn, 2002)).

23. There is evidence from 'input-output' statistical analyses on education in developing countries that textbooks substantially improve student learning and this has led to an emphasis on textbook production in development assistance programmes. There is currently only limited evidence on how textbooks are actually used by teachers and students, however, and less on their non-cognitive effects and societal impact (Benavot, 2002, p. 93-94).

24. See the Institute's website (www.gei.de) and publications. The Council of Europe has many activities in this field (see www.coe.int), as has UNESCO (see UNESCO, 1992; Pingel, 1999), which supports an International Textbook Research Network. See also the website of the European Standing Conference of History Teachers Associations (www.clioh.net).

25. This might be enriched by reference to Carol Gilligan's emphasis on the stronger development of the 'ethics of care' that she observed in girls and women, and to inter-cultural differences (Mulder, 1997).

26. See Miller & Affolter, 2002. Developmental stages for understanding the democratic ideal have been identified as: stage one, freedom to speak one's mind; stage two, listening to, taking the perspective of and having respect for other individuals and for

the needs of the majority; stage three, open dialogue, with special concern for the perspectives of minorities and the community as a whole (Power et al, 1989; Power, 1999).

27. Baxter (2001); Bruner (1960, 1966). The curriculum likewise follows the constructivist principle that cognitive development is stimulated through social interaction, working year by year within what Vygotsky (1978) called the 'zone of proximal development' — the problem-solving and learning that the child is ready to attain, given the help of peers or adults.

28. Pamela Baxter (personal communication).

29. Pamela Baxter (personal communication).

30. Pamela Baxter (personal communication).

31. Lederach (1994, p. 55) notes that 'The elicitive approach starts from the vantage point that training is an opportunity aimed primarily at discovery, creation and solidification of models that emerge from the resources present in a particular setting and respond to needs in that context'.

# CHAPTER IV
# A closer look at some programmes

In this chapter, we look in more detail at some educational programmes designed to develop skills and values that are supportive of conflict prevention and resolution, respect for human rights and humanitarian norms, active citizenship, and 'life-skills' for the health of oneself and others, including prevention of HIV/AIDS. The approach adopted here is to present some illustrative case studies, rather than to attempt a comprehensive review, and to identify some of the characteristics of successful programmes. The examples are taken to a considerable extent from countries affected by conflict, political transition or social crises. However, the issues raised are of wider application.

Programmes selected for presentation have mostly been the subject of an evaluation that is in the public domain. In each case study, we shall examine the origins of the programme; its rationale and goals; the teaching/learning model; the impact on classroom practice, teacher and student competencies; and dissemination and sustainability.

## PROGRAMMES FOCUSED ON ACQUISITION
## AND INTERNALIZATION OF SKILLS AND VALUES

We shall begin by looking at some programmes that focus primarily on the behavioural skills and values dimensions of our area of concern, rather than subject-matter content. These programmes will help us address the feasibility of promoting the acquisition and internalization of the pro-social skills, values and behaviours under consideration here. When a programme is specifically designed around skills and values, rather than mixed in with a heavy load of subject-matter content, it is easier to see whether the skills and values are acquired or not. There can be fewer excuses that teachers focused their time and attention on other things.[1]

The first case study concerns the former 'Eastern bloc' countries undergoing political transition, which have felt the need for renewal of their education systems. The focus of this programme, entitled *Reading and Writing for Critical Thinking,* was to develop higher-order cognitive skills of analysis, reflection and evaluation, in contrast to the previous situation under communist rule, when teachers and students were at the receiving end of a top-down approach to learning. The initiative was taken by a large NGO, the International Reading Association. The objective of the programme was to provide critical thinking skills as a foundation for democratic citizenship.

The second example is a programme established in Northern Ireland by a Quaker group working with the University of Ulster that attempts to give children a better understanding of how conflicts happen and how they can be resolved.[2] The programme has been recognized for its work on peer mediation in schools. The wider aim is for students to see the case for conflict resolution and reconciliation in their divided society.

Case study 3 describes an initiative taken by a UN agency, jointly with NGOs, the UNHCR peace education programme (later taken up by the Inter-Agency Network for Education in Emergencies) mentioned earlier, with its cyclic curriculum for the systematic development of skills and values for conflict prevention and peace throughout the years of schooling, as well as community workshops for youth and adults.

Case study 4 describes the Lions-Quest 'life-skills' programmes, developed in the United States but used internationally, that focus on preventive health behaviours and social responsibility.[3]

The success of these programmes, as indicated by external evaluation reports, shows that the goals of building support and skills for peace, tolerance and respect for other people are attainable, given the right conditions.

## PROGRAMMES FOCUSED ON RESPECT FOR HUMAN RIGHTS, HUMANITARIAN NORMS, ACTIVE CITIZENSHIP

Most programmes in this category incorporate substantial knowledge objectives alongside objectives of developing respect for others, conflict prevention and resolution, tolerance, etc. They face the possibility that the latter 'behavioural' objectives will be neglected in favour of conventional activities such as learning the names of human rights instruments and humanitarian conventions or the particularities of the national constitution. Some programmes focus on the student in his/her personal life and environment, and move on through local action projects to national and global concerns. Others are more focused on the constitutional, legal and political dimension, and approach the student's appreciation of values from there.

The mix of levels from personal to global (called 'nested layers' by Miller and Affolter, 2002) was illustrated in Chapter II by reference to Argentina's curriculum framework for Ethical and Citizenship Education. Cox (2002, p. 126) notes, however, the bias in the Latin American region towards academic rather than learning-by-doing approaches in this and other programmes, and the same problems are found in other regions. This 'default setting' of transmitting factual information rather than 'education for transformation' is a challenge for human rights and citizenship education everywhere.[4]

Even in the more 'developed' countries participating in the 1999 Civic Education Study in 28 countries, organized by the International Association for the Evaluation of Educational Achievement, school teachers admitted that their teaching methods were often not adapted to the concept they have of citizenship education.[5]

---

**Vision and reality**

Teachers tend to have a vision of civic education that emphasizes critical thinking, but they report that, in practice, their most frequent instructional mode involves transmission of factual knowledge through textbooks, recitation and worksheets. Teachers in many countries also say that **civic education would be improved if they had better materials, more subject-matter training and more instructional time.**

The first phase of the study, using case studies, concluded that civic education is a **low status subject** in many countries (Torney-Purta et al. 2001, p. 13-14; emphasis added).

---

A great deal of skill is needed to design curricula that involve the students at a personal level in terms of their identity and development of skills and values, while dealing with macro-level issues and structures. Holt (2001) has described how the Curriculum Corporation in Australia undertook extensive field-testing and re-writing so that its 'Discovering Democracy' programme would engage the minds and feelings of students.[6]

Case study 5 describes the support given by the Norwegian Refugee Council, an international NGO, to Education Ministries in the Caucasus, for the development of human rights education in primary schools. Case study 6 describes recent UNESCO support to a local NGO, the Kosovo Centre for Human Rights, also for human rights education in national schools.

Case study 7 introduces the programme *Exploring Humanitarian Law,* developed by the International Committee of the Red Cross (ICRC). This programme has been piloted in many countries and represents an important contribution to education for secondary students and in non-formal settings. There is a carefully planned sequence of activities that develop cognitive understandings and skills alongside values.

Case study 8 is from Northern Ireland, where the government announced in 1989 that *Education for Mutual Understanding* (EMU) would be introduced as a cross-cutting curriculum theme. This administratively simple approach led to disappointing results. However, the EMU initiative was the jumping off point for a new *citizenship* programme for secondary schools, with rather similar objectives. Both programmes are presented together. The importance of this case study is that it shows the problems and possibilities of education for reconciliation and citizenship in the context of a modern and relatively well-resourced education system.

Case study 9 is the *Global Education* initiative supported by UNICEF in several Arab states and Albania. This programme was well received by teachers and students even though they had limited experience of interactive education.

Case study 10 shows the effect of an experimental civics education programme in Romania using a more participative and thematic approach, as evidenced by the impact on students' attitudes and values.

Case study 11 describes the experience of the *Escuela Nueva* movement originating in Colombia. It shows that rural teachers with modest education can introduce a holistic approach to citizenship, provided that they are given appropriate training and support materials.


## HIV/AIDS EDUCATION

This section touches on the field of HIV/AIDS education, drawing on the evaluation of programmes in Eastern and Southern Africa commissioned by UNICEF and other sources.[7] The dilemma of teaching facts versus inculcating new behaviours is dramatically illustrated here. Increasingly, students already know many of the facts, but teachers find it hard to present lessons that engage students enough to change their responses to situations that endanger their own health and that of others.

Chapter IV closes optimistically with the conclusion that skills, concepts and values related to the goals in Chapter II can be inculcated by education programmes of the type presented in the case studies. But there are many conditions to be met. These are the subject of the lessons-learned analysis in Chapter V.

## Case study 1: The Reading and Writing for Critical Thinking Project (RWCT)

*Origins*. RWCT began in 1997 as a way of helping educators in the former 'Eastern bloc' develop critical thinking skills among students, after the 'top-down' approaches to education under the previous communist regimes. It grew out of discussions in 1995 between the International Reading Association, based in the USA, and the Open Society Institute founded by George Soros.[8] The Institute agreed to fund a 'Reading for Understanding' project developed by the Soros Romania Foundation that would help Hungarian and Romanian children understand each other better through the use of literature, stories, reading and writing. This led to a more formal programme proposal, RWCT, incorporating critical thinking and active learning, to be funded partly by Soros national foundations and partly by the Open Society Institute.

RWCT is an in-service teacher-training programme based on voluntarism at the level of individual teachers, who choose to participate in trainings provided by external volunteer trainers from the International Reading Association and by national trainers. In the start-up period, 1997-2000, more than 12,200 teachers completed RWCT training workshops in twenty-four countries throughout Eastern Europe and Central Asia, and others participated in short term seminars. The geographic coverage is now expanding.[9] The training covers educators at every grade level, from primary school to post-secondary and is not limited to specific subject areas. An evaluation conducted in 2000-2001 in the Czech Republic, Kyrgyzstan, Latvia and Macedonia indicated that the project was having a measurable impact on classroom practice (AIR, 2001).[10]

*Rationale and goals*. RWCT is based on the premise that school children who experience interactive learning processes and democratically structured classroom discussions, and are trained in critical thinking, will develop key skills and values for building an open and democratic society.

*Teaching/learning model*. The first step in the programme is the training of teachers in critical thinking and interactive pedagogy.[11] Lesson planning is structured in terms of Evocation, Realization of Meaning and Reflection (ERR). This model provides students with 'the time and means to actively integrate information with previously held beliefs and ideas so that their learning will be conceptualized and, consequently, more real and lasting' (Steele, 2000).

---

**The ERR model**

*Evocation:* used at the beginning of a lesson to help students evoke prior knowledge, sentiment or impressions and create a context for new learning.

*Realization of meaning:* students engage with the new material (whether reading, discussion, videotape, etc), integrate new knowledge with existing knowledge and consider its applicability in new situations.

*Reflection:* robust discussions, practical application of knowledge, generation of new ideas and concepts, open speculation about implications, students developing their own views and defending them (Steele, 2000).

---

Eight guidebooks for teachers were prepared in 1998, covering critical thinking, discussion, co-operative learning, lesson planning and assessment, written arguments and thoughtful reading. They are presented to teachers in four 4-day intensive workshops over the course of one academic year. In-service training sessions conclude with teachers developing implementation plans for immediate use of the new approach in their classrooms. Support is provided through monthly meetings with other RWCT teachers and some classroom mentoring. In-service training in the second year includes preparing participants to act as trainers in their turn.

The RWCT approach minimizes teacher-led classroom interactions such as lecturing, and encourages student-driven discussions and investigations. Teachers are expected to spend more time acting as mentors and facilitators, encouraging students to form original opinions, debate and choose rationally between competing ideas, work co-operatively to develop new ideas and solve problems. Students are encouraged to appreciate different points of view and recognize the ways in which people's backgrounds can influence their attitudes and perceptions (AIR, 2001).

*Impact on classroom practice, teacher and student competencies and values.* The 2001 evaluation included observation of classes with students in the fourth to eighth year of schooling. The evidence showed that there was more pupil-pupil interaction and less unidirectional teacher communication in classes taught by RWCT teachers than in comparable control classes. Moreover, 'RWCT teachers were observed to promote more higher-order thinking skills, substantive conversation and interest in the world outside the classroom than teachers in control groups. RWCT teachers were also more likely than their peers to organize classroom information to promote discussion and critical thinking, encourage pupils to consider multiple answers to problems, and wait for pupils to answer questions' (AIR, 2001).

While there is a possibility that the profile of teachers entering the programme might differ from the average, the research indicated that exposure to RWCT training led to increased integration of critical thinking principles into teachers' classroom practice year by year (as evidenced by comparison of teachers' classroom methods according to when they had first received training). The trained teachers themselves testified to the effect the training had had on their teaching methods.

---

**Impact on RWCT teachers**

It is difficult to fully articulate the dynamic change process set in motion by the program. It is palpable, observable and exciting. Participating educators become consumed by it. They come to believe in the process and its power of renewal for them as professional educators and human beings (Steele, 2000).

---

Primary and secondary school and college students who met with the evaluation team indicated that they were 'learning more' with RWCT teachers and appreciated the instructional methods.[12] RWCT pupils scored significantly higher on critical thinking assessments than pupils in the control groups, in terms of ability to form original opinions, choose rationally among competing ideas, solve problems and debate ideas responsibly.[13]

RWCT is thus an example of successful transformation of the methodology of teaching in terms of certain skills and values associated with democratic processes. It is not clear from the evaluation report, however, to what extent teachers systematically work to ensure the transferability of students' new skills and values from critical thinking in connection with school subjects to the wider issues of strengthening civil society, democracy and human rights, fulfilling the goal that 'schools will help young people become thoughtful, engaged members of a society in which differences are settled with debates and ballots, not brutality, hatred and so-called ethnic cleansing'.[14]

*Dissemination and sustainability.* The RWCT strategy involved a three-year start-up cycle. This was perhaps sufficient in countries with a well-educated teaching force, where the primary task was to initiate and legitimize a transformation of methodology. Four international educators who volunteered through the IRA travelled regularly to a given host country to train 20-40 national teachers to use RWCT strategies with their own students and then to become trainers. This has enabled large numbers of teachers to be reached. After the three-year cycle, the national project becomes autonomous, as an NGO, university centre or through a national affiliate of the International Reading Association. International RWCT certification standards have been developed for teachers and trainers and some national programmes offer training services to their Ministries of Education.

Strategically, the RWCT country co-ordinators have in some cases been able to influence national educational reform. For example:

- The new curriculum in the Czech Republic, and new standards for teaching in Latvia, included enhancement of pupils' critical thinking skills as a recommended instructional goal.
- The Education Ministry in Kyrgyzstan approved RWCT as an in-service professional development programme.
- RWCT teaching methods were incorporated into the teacher education programme at the Institute of Pedagogy, a major pre-service training institution in Macedonia. (AIR, 2001).

---

**Case study 2:**
**The Northern Ireland Quaker Peace Education Programme (QPEP)**

---

*Origins.* The 'Troubles' in Northern Ireland, low-level violence dating from 1967 but the product of centuries of history, led to many education initiatives designed to improve relations between Protestants and Catholics, in order to facilitate the cessation of violence and the establishment of some form of mutually acceptable governance. One of these initiatives, the Quaker Peace Education Programme (QPEP), is chosen for discussion here because of its skills-based approach and the good documentation available. In the 1980s, the Quaker community in Northern Ireland collected funds from private donations and charities to initiate an action-research programme on education for peace and mutual understanding, based at the Centre for the Study of Conflict at the University of Ulster. After six years, the project metamorphosed into the 'EMU-Promoting School Project' (the title refers to the cross-curricular theme of 'education for mutual understanding'), supported by the Department of Education for Northern Ireland and charitable sources.

*Rationale and goals.* One of the problems in Northern Ireland is that education has been largely segregated, with Protestant students attending government schools and Catholic students attending Catholic schools (which receive State support). This is the legacy of historical factors and often reflects the segregation of residential areas. The result is a high degree of distrust and misinformation between the two communities, feeding the ongoing political conflict and its paramilitary manifestations. Teachers themselves were often 'the naïve bearers of [sectarian] culture' (Skilbeck, 1976, cited in Arlow, 2003).

QPEP's aim was to find ways in which schools could sensitize students to the underlying causes of conflict, perceived as an iceberg of misunderstanding which needed to be tackled from the base rather than the symptoms that showed above the waterline. The focus was to be on action rather than on materials development, although the book of conflict resolution skills, *Wee people*, that QPEP produced was said to be a popular resource for teachers (Tyrrell, 1995, p. 59).

*Teaching/learning model.* The project began by assembling a team of volunteers, led by Jerry Tyrrell as the field worker (later the director). In the summer of 1988, they trained themselves using exercises that developed skills in communication, affirmation, co-operation and conflict resolution, drawing on the manual of the Kingston Friends Workshop Group (Bowers, 1984). This led to a pilot series of weekly workshops in a Catholic and a government (Protestant) school, running in parallel. The Project gradually extended its activities to a variety of settings.

In 1993, QPEP piloted a peer mediation approach with Year Seven pupils in the two Londonderry primary schools whose principals expressed an interest in this possibility, again as an action-research project led by the University. After each workshop (of 105 minutes' duration) the children's evaluations were reviewed to guide the planning of the next one. The training comprised six workshops, held weekly from October to December 1993. The workshops taught mediation skills in the context of the themes of affirmation, communication and co-operation. The children were increasingly involved in mediation role-plays, including small-group work. After the course, the classes selected between ten and fifteen children to be trained as peer mediators. Peer mediation was introduced in February 1994, and Year Seven children used it frequently. The peer mediation programme continued in subsequent years, and was extended to other interested schools.

*Impact on classroom practice, teacher and student competencies.* Teachers varied in their reaction to the class workshops, which were initially facilitated by QPEP staff. Staff support was found to be critical to the success and sustainability of the programme.

---

**Reaction of teachers**

There was a variety of responses from teachers to QPEP with regard to their participation in workshops. There were those who wanted QPEP to come in and work with the children but did not want to be present in the workshops at all. Those who had some experience in life-skills and/or group work relished the informality of the workshops. Some who had not had such experience were prepared to take part. (O'Neill, 1993, cited in Tyrrell, 1995)

---

Teachers found the peer mediation programme easier to understand than the earlier workshops, since it related to solving student complaints of the type they themselves had frequently to deal with. Reporting on the peer mediation programme, Tyrrell noted positive feedback from teachers and support staff. The class teachers as well as the lunch-time supervisors reported that playground incidents were reduced as a result of the programme.

Feedback from the class workshops introducing peer mediation indicated that students understood the importance of confidentiality and the significance of conflict resolution being achieved jointly by the conflicting parties. Feedback from the peer mediation experience itself was encouraging.

---

**Impact on students**

Among those chosen as mediators were a few whose behaviour had given cause for some concern. They proved excellent as mediators, and their behaviour improved noticeably. This suggested that the project had the potential to significantly address issues of behavioural change, through encouragement of children who were regularly in and out of conflict, to be mediators. It has been borne out by experience in other parts of the world that successful peer mediation schemes depend on this poacher-turned-gamekeeper factor. There was a consensus among the interviewed children that they had learned a lot about conflict and had developed confidence in dealing with it. (Tyrrell, 1995, p. 114-115)

---

*Dissemination and sustainability.* The QPEP programme evolved over the years. Some volunteers continued for several years while others came and went, such as those who were university students doing a work assignment. The initial three-year funding to QPEP was renewed for three years, and the activities subsequently continued under the new title of the EMU-Promoting School Project. Essentially the project provides support for schools that are willing to experiment with skills training for peace. The project has continued its work in peer mediation and maintained its action research approach, aiming at 'curriculum innovation and creation of a network of skilled practitioners' (Duffy, 2000).[15]

---

**Case study 3: The Inter-agency Peace Education Programme (PEP) initiated by UNHCR
(Office of the United Nations High Commissioner for Refugees),
and now linked to the Inter-agency Network for Education in Emergencies**

---

*Origins.* UNHCR has responsibility for education in refugee camps and settlements around the world, and for some internally displaced and returnee populations. The refugee situations of the 1990s, post-Cold War, often reflected tensions between ethnic groups, and it seemed important to equip conflict-affected populations with the tools for conflict prevention and peace-building, in support of more peaceful futures. Action research in the multi-ethnic refugee camps in Kenya led to a skills and values-based approach. Special funding obtained as a follow up to Graça Machel's (1996) *Report on the Impact of Armed Conflict on Children* was used to initiate school-based and community-based peace-education activities. The programme has spread to UNHCR-funded education programmes in several other countries.[16] PEP was designed around generic 'life-skills' that are applicable in a wide range of problematic situations, and the materials are not specific to refugees. After endorsement by UNICEF and UNESCO, the programme was 'donated' to the newly formed Inter-Agency Network for Education in Emergencies (INEE)[17] in 2001, to facilitate use of the materials by organizations not working in refugee situations.

---

**Participative programme development**

UNHCR's Education for Peace and Life-Skills Programme (PEP) began in 1998 in the refugee camps in Kenya, which house many ethnic groups and nationalities. This facilitated the development of materials of a generic nature, not linked to a particular national situation. Moreover, the programme was designed to encompass different religious groups, with the refugees in the Kakuma camps being predominantly Christian, and those in the Dadaab camps being mostly Muslim. Extensive consultations (about eighty) had been undertaken in 1997 by the peace education consultant who developed the programme, Pamela Baxter, covering all groups in the camps — often mini-workshops around the themes of peace and conflict and focused on the question 'Would you like your children to study peace education?' The answer was often 'Yes, but we would like to study it also.'[18] Hence the programme includes school-based courses and community workshops for youths and adults.

*Rationale and goals.* Peace education alone cannot build peace, since many other factors are involved. The initial goal of the programme was to develop an education programme that would *contribute* to peace and hamper the outbreak of violent conflict at personal, family, community and national level. It was hoped to strengthen the skills, values and understandings of peace and how to attain it, among the members of conflict-affected communities.[19] The objectives of the UNHCR programme were to develop 'knowledge, skills, values and attitudes that lead to behaviour that promotes peace and encourages conflict prevention and minimization' (Baxter, 2001, p. 28). It was believed that these same 'life-skills' and values could help promote gender-sensitive behaviour, minimize gender-based and sexual violence, help protect young people against peer pressures to adopt unsafe sexual behaviours, and lead to an understanding of the basic concepts of human rights.

*Teaching/learning model.* The conflict-prevention/peace-education programme developed by UNHCR and now associated with the Inter-Agency Network for Education in Emergencies (INEE) begins with the concept of a shared human identity ('similarities and differences' for the younger children, 'inclusion and exclusion' for older children and adults). Competencies are developed in the value context of peace between individuals and between larger groups. There is a constant blend of the cognitive, affective and psychological dimensions in the discussion and reflection following the group activity that introduces the session. The stimulus activity itself may be cognitive (e.g. solving a problem), affective (e.g. empathy), psychological (e.g. handling emotions) or a combination of these (such as role-play). The programme was designed to progressively build the skills, values and concepts for peace, following the sequence:

- similarities and differences;
- inclusion and exclusion;
- trust;
- one-way and two-way communication;
- perceptions;
- handling emotions;
- bias;
- empathy;
- co-operation;
- assertiveness;
- problem-solving;
- negotiation;
- mediation;
- reconciliation;
- human rights.[20]

PEP uses a whole community model, where circumstances permit.[21] The school-based programme is thus reinforced by what is happening in the community. In the refugee camps in Kenya, PEP includes:

- A *schools programme*, based on the pedagogic principles of a cyclic curriculum tailored to the stages of child development, as described in Chapter III above. It progressively introduces and deepens commitment to behavioural skills and values underlying peace, conflict resolution and related concepts, through weekly lessons for all school children, taught by specially trained peace-education teachers.
- A *community workshop programme* for youth and adults, comprising twelve three-hour sessions that draw on their life experience to create a toolbox for peace-building and pro-social behaviour.[22]
- *Public awareness activities* such as dramas, special functions, etc.

---

**An evaluator's view of the PEP model**

PEP is an education programme aiming at individual learning over time, through long-term programmes: a twelve-year programme in schools and an initial twelve-session community workshop reinforced by follow-up activities over the years. **PEP is first and foremost a skills acquisition programme** targeting various peace- building skills, such as:

- co-operation skills;
- communication skills — including enhanced listening, speaking skills and the skill of remaining silent;
- skills of trusting, of practising empathy;
- assertiveness skills deriving from enhanced self-esteem and self-image;
- the skill of taking increased individual and social responsibility — for one's life and decisions, and for other people;
- the skills of controlling emotions;
- mediation skills (a conflict-resolution skill, together with problem-solving, negotiation, and reconciliation skills) derived from an increased attitude of tolerance and open-mindedness. (Obura, 2002; emphasis in original)

---

PEP is almost entirely activity and discussion-based, to avoid the tendency towards rote learning or 'book learning' that is widespread in many countries. Since participative and interactive activities are critical to the theme of the present study, an example of a typical lesson structure and activity is given below. PEP uses this type of 'acting', role-plays or dramas extensively, to help students internalize the skills and values concerned. The actual content of the role plays is generated by the participants, which creates portability between settings.[23] PEP provides a safe space for practice of new behaviours and trial of new ideas before using them in everyday life and perhaps in an ethnically divided and/or post-conflict society.

Because of the skills that teachers need to handle an activity-based programme and open-ended class discussion on unfamiliar topics, PEP uses teachers specially selected for their aptitude for such work. In Kenya it was possible to hire full-time peace-education teachers, providing them with a ten-day initial training, followed by a ten-day training in each of the two succeeding vacations.[24] When possible, PEP advisors provide in-school training and support, as well as holding monthly professional development meetings.

## Example of a PEP lesson: Inclusion and Exclusion (Grade 8)

**Lesson 4:** *You don't belong*

### Objectives
- To help the students understand themselves and where they fit into society
- To help the students understand the motivation that leads to conflict.

### Teaching tips
- Remind the students to be considerate of other classes, if the activity is outdoors
- Explain to the students that they will be doing an activity to demonstrate exclusion
- Be sure to allow the students who were excluded to talk if they wish after the activity
- Remind all the students that this is a demonstration and that nobody should hold these negative feelings in their heart.

### Question bank
- How did you feel when nobody would talk to you?
- Did you feel that you were being rude when you ignored the people who didn't belong?
- Was it easier once you understood the rules of the group?
- How do you feel now about people that you have been rude to in the past?
- Do you think you now have more understanding about how other people feel when they are excluded?
- What will you do in the future to make sure that people are not excluded?

### Teacher instructions
- There is preparation for this lesson
- Make a small set of cards or slips of paper with stars, etc., on them
- There should be enough cards for half the class.

**Directions and method**

- Divide the class into two. Separate the two groups so you can talk to each group
- Tell the first group that they belong to a culture where people give each other cards before they speak
- If someone tried to talk to them without giving a card, they are obviously rude and should be ignored
- Ask this group to use their cards (give one to each person) and talk to each other
- Tell the second group to go and make friends with as many people as they can
- Watch the activity and then quietly give a card to somebody from group 2 and check to see if they understand the significance of the card
- Stop the activity and ask people how they felt
- This time take the second group and give them a nonsense phrase as the introduction to conversation
- Repeat as above.

**Discussion**

- Discuss with the students that the feelings that each group had when they were excluded are the same for all people who are excluded
- Exclusion generally leads to mistrust and a lack of communication. Both of these are causes of conflict.

**Conclusion**

- Remind the students that peace is a complex subject and that it has many parts. Peace can only be achieved when all the parts work together.

---

*Impact on classroom practice, teacher and student competencies.* Anna Obura's evaluation of the PEP programme in the refugee camps in Kenya (Obura, 2002) showed that some refugee teachers were able to facilitate class discussions well, moving easily from the practical exercises, such as active listening, differing perceptions of a picture, problem-solving exercises, etc., to the intended learning outcomes about respect for social diversity, win-win solutions and so on. Others found it more difficult to facilitate the discussion part of the lesson. Considering the lack of professional preparedness of most of the refugee teachers, and the high levels of teacher turnover in the camps, this is not surprising. The evaluation recommended strengthening of the in-service training and support. Specific findings included:

- Most teachers needed urgent upgrading on *questioning skills;*
- Practice on organizing the 'activities' was needed by some teachers;
- Teachers needed to *name the skill* of the lesson, and plan for appropriate skill-practice time in each lesson;

- Focus could be given to skills practice and out-of-class practice through students writing 'skill memos' (see box below);
- Teachers should *mention ethnic/sensitive issues in class* instead of skirting around them;
- More use should be made of music (especially at lower primary level), poetry and drama;
- More use should be made of *pair work* (especially where there are overcrowded classes);
- Special arrangements should be made to cope with oversized lower primary classes (sometimes over 100 pupils), with more emphasis on music and activities and simplified discussion;
- Much more teacher training was needed on gender sensitivity;
- Trainee and inexperienced teachers should *observe the best peace education teachers;*
- Teachers should have access to *more background reading and reference materials;*
- *Budget allocations for teacher/facilitator trainings were inadequate* and should be increased.

Several of these recommendations are relevant to many programmes working towards the goals of peace, respect for human rights, active citizenship and preventive health, including HIV/AIDS prevention.

---

**Sample student's skill memo (as suggested by Obura, 2002)**

*SKILL TO PRACTISE:*   Say good things, don't spread bad gossip.

*MY TASK THIS WEEK:*   SAY ONE GOOD THING PUBLICLY ABOUT A CHILD FROM ANOTHER ETHNIC GROUP

*WHAT MUST I LEARN?*   Saying good things about people builds peace. Spreading bad information destroys peace.

---

The evaluation was primarily an impact study, rather than a tracer survey of students who had completed the school or adult course.[25] It was difficult to identify the contribution of peace education to some of the changes in the camp, but Anna Obura, an experienced evaluator, found a correlation between the introduction of PEP and the reduction of violence. [26]

PEP achievements in Kakuma and Dadaab refugee camps in Kenya (1998-2002)

- Positive impact on skills acquisition/ peace-building practices observed
- Increased confidence and skills of PEP educators
- Some outstanding individual educators with no more than twelfth-grade schooling
- Daily demonstration in schools of non-violent, supportive pupil/teacher relations in a context rife with corporal punishment
- Positive impact contributing (with other measures) to more peace in the life of the camps:
  - Conflict prevention and prevention of escalation
  - Resolution of small problems, quarrels and fights
  - Containing small disputes
  - Improved camp security, less crime, safety levels increased
  - More/better inter-group interaction and integration
  - Emerging spontaneous/unplanned effects: refugee initiatives in the camps, initial networking for course development in the home country (Obura, 2002).

*Dissemination and sustainability.* The programme in the refugee camps in Kenya has been sustained thanks to earmarked donor funding, and it was possible to add a specially trained peace-education teacher to the approximately twenty teachers in the typical primary school. The task of 'mainstreaming' has been difficult. The original intention was that NGOs implementing school programmes for UNHCR would routinely include peace-education teachers and facilitators in the education budget. Recent years have seen such intense downward pressure on UNHCR budgets, however, that this has proved difficult.

The programme has been introduced for displaced or returnee communities in several other countries in Africa, linked to UNHCR-funded NGO or government educational programmes. Many implementation difficulties have arisen, however, linked to instability (which has repeatedly disrupted the Liberian programme and the start-up of programmes in Guinea and Sierra Leone), funding problems and bureaucratic hurdles.

The most fundamental problem when introducing the programme in a new setting is perhaps the difficulty of gaining that extra period in the timetable required for PEP activities to be effective. Attempts in some locations to 'integrate' the programme into existing subjects have run into the obvious problems of lack of teacher skills and pressure on teachers to concentrate on 'covering the syllabus' to prepare for examinations.

The materials and methodologies themselves, developed in East Africa, were found by West African practitioners to be suitable there. Elements of the programme have more recently been taken to Sri Lanka, Kosovo, and Afghan refugees in Pakistan. The materials were designed from the beginning to be generic and do not refer to any specific country, or to refugees. They therefore constitute a useful resource both for those practitioners looking for a programme that can be used quickly with minimal adaptation and for those looking for an input into autonomous programme development. At the time of writing, the materials are being upgraded and extended through inter-agency co-operation between UNESCO and UNHCR, with a view to making them more widely available as a resource for curriculum renewal.

---

**Case study 4: Lions-Quest 'Skills for growing' (grades K-5),
'Skills for adolescence' (grades 6-8) and 'Skills for action' (grades 9-12)**

---

*Origins.* The Quest programme dates from 1975 when Rick Little, as a 19-year-old college student, faced a personal crisis and began a 'quest' to help other young people develop skills to cope with life's problems. Quest received an initial grant in 1977 and launched 'Skills for living', for high-school-age youth, based on the philosophy of actively involving the family, school and local community. Lions Clubs International supported the programme from 1984. [27]

Quest's life-skills programmes have been the subject of some sixty research studies, which 'have demonstrated their effectiveness in changing the knowledge, attitudes and beliefs that lead to violence and substance abuse, and in strengthening the factors that protect young people from harmful, high-risk behaviours'. While the programme works primarily with US-based partner organizations, there is now international outreach. Each year, Lions-Quest programmes reach over two million young people in 30 countries, primarily through school-based initiatives. To date, more than 200,000 teachers and other adults have been trained to implement the programmes in school and community settings, reaching more than twelve million children.[28] The Quest initiative is in line with the framework of cognitive, affective, social and psychological objectives developed by CASEL, the 'Collaborative to Advance Social and Emotional Learning', presented in Chapter III above.

*Rationale and objectives.* Quest's programmes began as a response to the problems of American adolescents, but expanded to cover all grades of schooling in order to increase their effectiveness, especially in response to intensified problems of drug abuse and violence in schools.

---

**Building resilience**

Lions-Quest programmes build resiliency in young people by focusing on two primary outcomes:
–   Helping young people develop positive social behaviours such as self discipline, responsibility, good judgment, and the ability to get along with others
–   Helping young people develop positive commitments to their families, schools, peers and communities, including a commitment to leading healthy, drug-free lives.

---

*Teaching/learning model*. Lions-Quest programmes are 'values-based' and provide:

> sequentially designed, grade-specific classroom materials that teach competencies such as self-discipline, communication/collaboration, problem-solving, co-operation, resistance and conflict management skills. The lessons are highly interactive, and through guided skill practice, discussions and service-learning, students practise and apply the skills they are learning.

The modules in *Skills for Adolescence*, for example, comprise:

* Entering the teen years;
* Building self-confidence through better communication;
* Learning about emotions — developing competence in self-assessment and self-discipline;
* Friends — improving peer relationships;
* Developing critical thinking skills for decision making;
* Setting goals for healthy living;
* Developing one's potential.

The programmes are flexible, designed to be incorporated into traditional subjects or taught separately, especially at middle and high school levels. Parent and community involvement is a key feature of the programme. Resources for the adolescence programme, for example, include a Curriculum Manual, a Teacher's Resource Guide, a student book entitled *Changes and challenges*, a parents' book entitled *The surprising years: understanding your changing adolescent* and a guide to leading parent meetings called *Supporting young adolescents*. Representatives from Lions and other service organizations, business, law enforcement and youth organizations are encouraged to participate in training workshops, school-climate activities, panel discussions, service projects and parent meetings, and to provide financial support (WHO, 1994, p. 14).

*Impact on classroom practice, teacher and student competencies and values.* Researchers, using pre-and post-course tests and/or control groups, have reported many positive outcomes:

*Attitudes*
- *Skills for growing*: improved attitudes towards risks of harmful substances, positive peer relationships, positive self-concept, decision-making, conflict management
- *Skills for adolescence*: improved attitudes towards harm from alcohol and other drugs, taking responsibility for their own behaviour, disapproval of peers taking drugs

*Knowledge*
- *Skills for adolescence*: improved knowledge about risks of alcohol and other drugs, improved literacy and numeracy achievement

*Behaviour*
- *Skills for growing*: more positive health-oriented behaviours
- *Skills for adolescence*: lower self-reported rates of alcohol and tobacco use, lower predictions of use of alcohol and drugs in the next thirty days, better school attendance.[29]

*Dissemination and sustainability.* Lions-Quest is a not-for-profit organization that works through partnerships with many networks serving schools and youth programmes, including associations of school administrators, school principals, parent/teacher associations, juvenile and family-court judges, and youth leadership, as well as voluntary organizations such as Lions Clubs International that provide financial and other support. It maintains a referral list of educators in the US who can provide information and guidance to interested schools. Lions Club International, with 1.4 million members from 186 countries and territories, provides a tool of international outreach.

---

**Case study 5: Norwegian Refugee Council Human Rights Education Initiative in the Caucasus**

---

*Origins.* The Norwegian Refugee Council (NRC) has supported human rights education in the Southern Caucasus since 1995, working through the Ministries of Education and developing core groups of national trainers. The programme was introduced in Armenia in 1996, in Georgia in 1997 and in Azerbaijan in 1998. By 2001, when an evaluation was conducted, the programme had reached an estimated 30,000 school children. Some 3,717 people had been trained, of whom 74% were school teachers, while others were school directors and ministry personnel. In Armenia, four counties were given priority because of the relatively large numbers of internally displaced people and refugees, while in Georgia most regions were represented in the programme, and in Azerbaijan eight districts had been reached.

*Rationale and objectives.* The programme reflects the mandate of the Norwegian Refugee Council to assist refugees and internally displaced persons (Midttun, 1999). The period after the dissolution of the Soviet Union represented an historic opportunity to influence school curricula and processes towards the ideals of human rights as well as the protection of refugees and the victims of internal displacement.

*Teaching/learning model.* The programme was based on local adaptation of a *Teacher's Resource Book for Human Rights Education*, developed by the Norwegian team, who also conducted initial and refresher trainings for national education officials and trainers. The resource book introduces the themes of basic needs, the three generations of human rights, children's rights, conflict prevention and management, encouraging participative methods of teaching. Textbooks for children were produced at country level. The programme was made available to schools on an optional basis, covering grades one to three of primary school in Armenia (with the Education Ministry developing a programme for higher grades), grades four, nine and eleven in Georgia, and grades three and four in Azerbaijan.

---

**Introducing participatory teaching of human rights**
A main principle in the Human Rights Education programme is the correspondence between the content and how the subject is taught. [...] The subject has to be adapted to the child's cognitive and social development and not be presented in a traditional abstract and non-participatory way. A participatory approach represents in itself a new challenge to teachers, children and parents in Southern Caucasus.

Academically the Soviet school was of a high standard [but] the school structure was, and still is, authoritarian and the relationship between teachers and students is hierarchical. The same relationship prevails between children and parents. [...] On the other hand, human rights issues are gaining momentum. Parents hear about it on TV and want to know more[...] (Johannessen, 2002).

---

*Impact on classroom practice, teacher and student competencies and values.* Eva Johannessen's evaluation in 2002 found positive results in terms of teaching methods, as well as human rights concepts, despite the authoritarian traditions in the classroom and families. However, there was great variation between schools, with some teachers using participatory methods though having a limited understanding of human rights, others teaching human rights in a traditional way, and others using methodology that matched the human rights content. In schools where several teachers and the principal had been trained there was more impact than in schools where only one or two teachers had been trained. Teacher training by national trainers followed the intended model, including the use of games, exercises, role-play and discussions, but the time available for training was limited in relation to the changes envisaged for teaching methods. Various methods for follow-up support and training were being developed by the core teams in the three countries.

Although the programme took the position that human rights education should be inherent in all subjects, with a more specific focus in subjects such as history and civics, the majority of the 2,271 teachers who had been trained under the programme found it easier or more convenient to teach the new material as a separate subject. Integration in the existing school programme was found mostly in Armenia, where the intervention was in the early stages of primary school, and integration was easier.

The children told the evaluator they liked the human rights classes because they were allowed to express their opinions. However, this was limited by the culture, and the evaluator spent a considerable amount of time discussing children's attitudes to being hit by teachers and their uncritical acceptance of rules and decisions made by teachers and parents. She felt there were rules in the classroom that needed to be discussed and that there was a long way to go before children were looked upon as competent and capable of taking responsibility for their learning process.

In Armenia, the government has made human rights education compulsory as a separate subject, and NRC has been asked to focus on grades one to three. In Georgia and Azerbaijan, the subject is not compulsory although it will become part of the new middle-school civics education in Georgia.

*Dissemination and sustainability.* NRC helped train a 'core group' of national trainers in each country. As of 2002, the core groups comprised six people in Armenia, eight people in two groups in Georgia, and three people in Azerbaijan. The core groups were struggling with the dual tasks of strengthening the performance of teachers they had already trained and extending the outreach of the programme.

As part of the phase-out programme from the Norwegian side, the core group in Armenia had constituted itself as a 'Fund for Human Development and Human Rights', while in Azerbaijan the core group was considering a similar approach and planned to continue working closely with other international and national organizations, such as the local 'Children's Rights Defence League'. In Georgia, the Tbilisi core group was directly under the Ministry of Education, and planned to continue its work in connection with the Institute of Teacher Training.

Eva Johannessen recommended a longer time-frame before phasing out NRC support, given that much project time had inevitably been taken up with establishing co-operation at Ministry level, organizing local core groups and producing education materials, before implementation began. Based on the experience in the Caucasus, she recommended that in future initiatives, preparation for local implementation mechanisms should be planned from the beginning, alongside the introductory workshops on human rights education and participatory methods for senior managers. A local co-ordinator should be engaged and core groups responsible for training established in parallel with the introductory workshops (Johannessen, 2002). *Establishment of an effective and representative 'core group' of this kind is critical to programme success* (see Chapter V below).

---

### Case study 6: Training of Teachers in Democracy and Human Rights Project, Peja Region, Kosovo

---

*Origins.* The Kosovo Centre for Human Rights (KCHR) is an NGO founded in July 2000, which seeks to promote human rights and human rights education in Kosovo. Its teacher training project was a joint initiative with UNESCO, supported by the United Nations Mission in Kosovo (UNMIK), the Finnish Human Rights Project and several donors. Between September and November 2001, 120 teachers were trained in five-day seminars held in the five municipalities of the Peja region. The teachers prepared materials for twenty lessons for grades eight and nine of primary school. The programme was introduced in fifty-five schools, to 7,000 students.

*Rationale and objectives.* The project was created as a way of building knowledge, skills and attitudes that are supportive of human rights and democracy throughout the Peja region, one of the most war-affected areas of Kosovo. The involvement of the Teacher-Training Institute based in the region was seen as a way of preparing for outreach to other parts of Kosovo.

The project was designed to train school directors and teachers in human rights education in a way that they are able to take into account all these aspects of implementing human rights education in their schools. The main target for implementation during the project was, however, on human rights education teaching, either during different subject lessons or as a special course at seventh and eighth grades of primary school (UNESCO & KCHR, 2003).

*Teaching/learning model.* The teaching/learning materials and activities were organized under twelve concepts identified by Kosovar teachers: peace; democracy; security; justice and human rights framework; ethics; solidarity; responsibility; child rights; tolerance; compromise; identity and minority rights.

In most of the schools, teachers arranged a separate lesson period for human rights education, as well as including human rights elements in other classes. A minority of participating schools simply included human rights issues in normal classes.

*Impact on classroom practice, teacher and student competencies and values.* An evaluation was conducted by the international and national trainers in early 2003, after the programme had been in operation for a year, mainly through discussions with and questionnaire completion by staff and students. Teachers in the Klina municipality said they received very positive feedback from the students and parents. Active methods, such as role-plays, simulations and visits to outside institutions, had been successful. School directors in this municipality felt that:

> All the topics are important and some topics are part of the civics curriculum. For implementing human rights education there is no need for a separate subject, but extra time is needed, for instance one weekly hour discussing human rights issues.

---

**Feedback from teacher groups in the Istog municipality**

More than 50% of teachers think that human rights education can be spread through the existing lessons. [....] Other proposals:
- Human rights education should start from an earlier age, at pre-schools, through a game [...] its contents become more familiar and raise the interest of students up to ninth grade (more than 70% of respondents make this proposal)
- Human rights education should be learned by including it in a new lesson that could have a positive impact, which could be called 'Children's education on human rights protection' (more than 60% agreed on this proposal) (UNESCO & KCHR, 2003).

---

*Dissemination and sustainability*. The 2003 evaluation led to an awareness of three modalities for insertion in the curriculum: a separate course, a teaching module inside one subject and as a cross-curriculum issue. Experience was gained in new pedagogical approaches and student/teacher relationships, as well as healing of the trauma of war:

> The project did experimental work in one of the core areas of the curriculum reform. The project experiences will be valuable for both the curriculum development and the reform of teacher training. (UNESCO & KCHR, 2003)

The KCHR will work to build on these beginnings (Paolo Fontani, personal communication).

---

| Case study 7: Exploring Humanitarian Law (EHL) |
| --- |

Origins. The Exploring Humanitarian Law (EHL) project was initiated in 1998 by the International Committee of the Red Cross (ICRC), in close association with the Education Development Center (EDC) and with the active participation of educators and students in twenty countries throughout the world. The purpose of the project was to design core learning materials for global use among young people aged thirteen to eighteen. It represented an educational response to a range of violence, including armed conflict and urban violence involving youth.

---

**Consultative approach**

EHL project development work was started in 1999 with the establishment of a network of some fifteen sites around the world to identify interest and set up an informal group of contacts. Once established, the groups provided the research and curriculum development process with information from the viewpoint of the local learning environment, conducting some thirty-five focus group discussions with young people and probing perceptions of humanitarian limits, human dignity in war and relevance of education in humanitarian law. Associated sites have also been reviewing and/or trying out prototype materials with youth groups and giving critical input to feed into the process of curricular development. This consultation has largely confirmed the working hypothesis, [...] that ethical explorations of humanitarian law and the experience of war are perceived as relevant and meaningful learning, regardless of the local experience of armed conflict (Tawil, 2000).

A resource pack of field-tested materials was issued in 2001/2002, in English, Arabic, French and Spanish (ICRC, 2001), with translations into ten other languages following quickly and a further nine translations expected by the end of 2003.

---

*Rationale and objectives.* The programme seeks to develop knowledge and understanding of international humanitarian law (IHL) and related humanitarian issues in order to prevent and limit violations of IHL and of the 'hard core' of human rights. EHL also helps youth to understand the importance of regulatory systems in protecting life and human dignity in times of armed conflict and, by extension, in everyday life.

---

**Why teach EHL?**

Exploring Humanitarian Law is made up of a series of explorations that aim to improve understanding of humanitarian issues related to situations of conflict. It thus contributes to education in global citizenship, rights education and the development of life-skills. It may also contribute to learning in specific academic subject areas, such as law, history, social studies and philosophy at the secondary level. States party to the Geneva Conventions have an obligation to spread knowledge of international humanitarian law (IHL) as widely as possible, including to civil society and youth. IHL can contribute to the common 'international' core of basic education. IHL education has a unique contribution to make to citizenship education at the local, national and international levels.[30]

---

The learning goals of EHL are to help young people adopt the principles of humanitarian behaviour in their daily lives, and to show positive changes in:

- Awareness of humanitarian norms, limits to permissible behaviour, and protections, during situations of armed conflict;
- Understanding of the multiple perspectives of those involved in situations of armed conflict and the potential complexity of applying IHL in real-life situations;
- Interest in international current events and humanitarian issues at local, national and international level;
- Capacity to view conflict situations at home and abroad from a humanitarian perspective based on respect for and protection of life and human dignity;
- Involvement in community service, promoting humanitarian attitudes and helping the most vulnerable members of society.[31]

*Teaching/learning model.* The programme requires the teacher to *explore* the subject matter alongside the students as a facilitator, modeling the ways to ask questions and handle concepts in this field. Communication skills are developed, through listening, discussing, debating and group work, while analytical skills are developed through interpretation of rules, identification of consequences of actions, problem-solving and analysis of dilemmas, especially in times of danger and conflict. Critical thinking skills are developed through requiring justification for students' ideas, confronting them with alternatives, asking open-ended questions, and requiring students to actively contribute to class discussion. 'Life-skills' are strengthened through discussing the application of social/interpersonal and cognitive skills to life situations especially in times of conflict that require difficult choices.

Cross-cutting skills and values are developed throughout the course through practice in disagreeing respectfully, brainstorming, perspective taking, role playing, story telling and analysis, dilemma analysis, identifying and tracing consequences, problem analysis and identifying solutions, needs assessment, estimating scope, estimating effort, working in groups, planning and journal writing.[32]

The course consists of twenty lesson units that can be taught as a separate topic or included under existing subjects. The lesson units draw on exciting stories of humanitarian acts, 'voices from war', photos, case studies of war crimes (notably the killings at My Lai), and 'dilemma scenarios'. Themes include 'what can bystanders do?'; the impact that one courageous person can have on others; codes of warfare over time; Henry Dunant's reactions to the Battle of Solferino and the founding of the Red Cross; the Geneva Conventions; the suffering of child soldiers; the campaign against anti-personnel mines; and the perspectives of combatants, prisoners of war and civilians caught up in difficult war-related situations. The course is structured in seven modules (see box).

---

**Curriculum of EHL**

*Module:*

| | |
|---|---|
| 1. Introductory exploration: | Limits to armed conflict; human dignity |
| 2. The humanitarian perspective: | Bystander; humanitarian act; social pressure |
| 3. Limits in armed conflict: | Limits to actions permissible during war; protection of civilians and non-combatants; human rights; needs of children; indiscriminate weapons; ripple effect |
| 4. The law (IHL) in action: | Violation; civilian/combatant distinction; chain reaction |
| 5. Ensuring justice (under IHL): | Implementation and enforcement of IHL; civilian/combatant distinction; illegal orders; social pressure; individual responsibility; leadership responsibility |
| 6. Responding to the consequence of war: | Basic needs; non-material needs; refugees, displaced persons; neutrality; impartiality |
| 7. Closing exploration: | Planning and implementing a project that promotes human dignity (ICRC, 2001). |

*Impact on classroom practice, teacher and student competencies and values.* The course is being introduced on a pilot basis in many countries where experiential approaches to education are new, meaning that teachers need intensive training in methodology as well as the unfamiliar content of IHL. Alma Baccino-Astrada, ICRC adviser for the programme in Latin America, notes that 'both the authorities and the teachers/instructors taking part in the programme require a *higher level of training in teaching techniques and humanitarian law than for a "traditional" programme* or project' (emphasis added). The approach used is to provide intensive training of a group of teachers, head teachers and administrators, and for the newly trained teachers to apply the programme in their own schools. More workshops of this type are needed to train new groups of teachers, still using international expertise, but with the role of ICRC progressively diminishing. After the programme has been in operation for some time, national trainers can be identified from among the pilot school teachers. The ICRC needs to give substantial support over the critical first two years of a programme, Baccino-Astrada (2003) advises, to ensure that the 'teething problems' of working with such a new and complex subject area can be overcome.

*Dissemination and sustainability.* EHL is designed to be adopted by Ministries of Education for use in schools, drawing on the support of the ICRC and national Red Cross and Red Crescent Societies, as well as being suited to non-formal workshops conducted by organizations catering to young people. 'The strategic goal is that EHL becomes fully accepted and integrated as part of basic education in the formal secondary school curricula across the world.'[33] The network of participating sites as of 2002-2003 includes thirteen countries or regions in Western Europe, fifteen in Eastern Europe, seventeen in the Middle East, thirteen in Africa and thirteen in the Americas. Of these, twenty-one sites had reached 'Phase Three', in which the Ministry of Education had made a commitment, teacher training for experimental classes is completed and the classes are ongoing. Another fifteen sites had completed Phase Two, the training of pilot teachers. As many as twenty-seven countries or regions had educators who have reached the level of 'International Master Trainers'. This *systematic and phased approach to innovation* can be taken as a model for other organizations working to promote education for peace, respect for human rights, active citizenship and preventive health, including HIV/AIDS prevention.

> **Case study 8: Northern Ireland—Education for Mutual Understanding, and Education for Local and Global Citizenship**

*Origins.* As noted earlier, the education system in Northern Ireland comprises mainly schools that are largely Protestant or largely Catholic, which tends to reinforce the Catholic-Protestant divide. The Department of Education for Northern Ireland was asked in 1975 to take steps to improve relations between the Protestant and Catholic communities. It supported a wide range of initiatives, leading to the idea of 'Education for Mutual Understanding' (EMU). In 1989, the new 'national curriculum' specified that EMU should become an integral part of all school programmes from 1992 onwards, as a 'cross-cutting theme' alongside themes such as Cultural Heritage.[34]

The Belfast (Good Friday) Agreement in April 1998 called for reconciliation, tolerance and mutual trust between the two religious groups and respect for human rights. A Ministerial Working Group examined ways for schools to promote these goals. Their 1999 report, *Towards a culture of tolerance: education for diversity,* advocated that schools should teach and reinforce the values of pluralism, social justice, human rights and responsibilities, and democracy. Concurrently, the School of Education at the University of Ulster set up the Social, Civic and Political Education Project (SCPE) in a trial group of twenty-five schools at lower secondary level. SCPE evolved into an official pilot project of the Council for Curriculum, Examinations and Assessment (CCEA), with the title of Local and Global Citizenship. 'Education for Local and Global Citizenship' is being introduced into lower secondary classes (grades six to eight) in Northern Ireland on a phased basis, over the period 2003/4 to 2008/9.

*Rationale and goals.* Despite the long history of inter-community conflict, the EMU initiative did not enjoy universal support, since some people saw it as having a political agenda (Smith & Robinson, 1996). In this environment, the education authorities offered a cautiously worded definition with minimal political overtones: 'Education for Mutual Understanding is about self-respect and respect for others, and the improvement of relations between people of differing cultural traditions.' The objectives for student learning were likewise expressed in a very general form, that could raise few objections: fostering respect for self and others; appreciating interdependence; understanding conflict; understanding cultural traditions (Smith & Robinson, 1996).

This lack of specificity regarding objectives and curriculum was one of the weaknesses of EMU (see below), and the new citizenship programme has a more specific approach.

> **Characteristics of the Local and Global Citizenship Programme**
>
> First, it is future orientated. Second, it is based on human rights principles. Third, it is open-ended. It asks young people to imagine a perfect world in the light of their understanding of human rights principles and then it seeks to help them to narrow the gap between the reality of today and the ideal of their perfect world. In that sense, it aims to be transformative but without being prescriptive about the outcome. (Arlow, 2001)

*Teaching/learning models.* Education for Mutual Understanding was introduced by 'Education Order' and constitutes an example of a legislative approach to curriculum reform. All schools and teachers were legally obliged to incorporate mutual understanding into their programmes of study by a certain date. Some general guidance was provided, but not specific classroom programmes or substantial in-service training (DENI, 1989; NICED, 1989). In 1996, further guidance was issued, with suggestions on how cross-curricular themes could be developed in the different Key Stages (levels) of schooling. Examples of good practice were provided, however, rather than a systematic curriculum framework (CCEA, 2000).

Schools have been free to design their own programmes, and many chose to undertake *inter-school visits* as a tangible manifestation of their commitment to EMU. These visits were encouraged under the Cross-Community Contact Scheme introduced in 1987, which was designed to encourage schools and youth groups to bring together young people from across the community through ongoing, constructive and collaborative activities that would lead to greater mutual understanding (DENI, 1990). Activities include single-day contact activities outside the school on an education visit or fieldwork; contact in each others' schools; and joint work in a residential setting for several days. Rather surprisingly, given the level of confrontation between the two communities, most parents were said to be supportive of this approach (Smith & Dunn, 1990). Core funding has been provided by the government to voluntary reconciliation groups that were active in supporting community relations initiatives in schools, reaching 717 schools (59%) in 2000/2001.[35] However, the impact of the 'contact' programmes based on short-term inter-personal contact has been questioned, given the entrenched nature of the conflict between the Catholic and Protestant communities (Smith & Robinson, 1996, p. 45; Duffy, 2000, p. 24-25).

The new Local and Global Citizenship model has a more structured approach than EMU. It is built around thematic areas that include finding ways to move beyond inter-communal conflict and towards active citizenship:

- diversity and inclusion;
- human rights and social responsibilities;
- equality and justice;
- democracy and active participation.

According to Arlow (2001):

> each of these areas is conceived as being problematic. It is to be investigated rather than taught didactically, [...] in local, national/European and global contexts. The thematic areas are investigated through specific issues, chosen by the teachers and sometimes by the students. [...] It is a communal rather than a purely individual process.

Consideration of diversity and inclusion leads on to ways to manage emotions and seek solutions to conflict and to issues of justice, laws, rights and values, and democratic ways of handling conflicting positions (Arlow, 2003). The programme was designed with the participation of practising teachers and is introduced through in-service teacher training.

*Impact on classroom practice, teacher and student competencies and values*
Education for Mutual Understanding. The 1996 evaluation indicated teachers' difficulties with EMU, especially the lack of training that might have helped them to deal with the politically sensitive and 'emotional' issues related to the conflict in Northern Ireland.

---

**Northern Ireland teachers' difficulties with EMU**

*Most teachers have a repertoire of teaching methods and strategies which are valuable and consistent with the aims and objectives of EMU (for example, small-group work which encourages interaction and co-operation between pupils; experience of working within mixed ability groups; and opportunities for pupils to have direct experience of democratic, consensual and other forms of decision-making).*

*However, it became clear that many teachers would welcome training and support which would strengthen their confidence in the emotive and affective aspects to learning which come to the fore through themes such as EMU and Cultural Heritage. In part, this would mean that teachers have opportunities to consider how their own values, attitudes and cultural background influence what and how they teach. Another dimension might involve extended practical experience of the dynamics of discussion within culturally diverse groups[...]*
Teachers face the challenge of how to address divisive issues constructively and with sensitivity, so that the emotional as well as the cognitive basis for conflict is

---

acknowledged. For example, it is not just interpretations of Irish History which can be disputed and controversial. Deciding whether to challenge a pupil who has just made a sectarian comment may be just as controversial and potentially more explosive if handled badly. This implies that staff need opportunities to:

- Identify explicitly topics which relate directly to Northern Ireland within various programmes of study;
- Anticipate where controversy regarding these may arise;
- Accumulate direct experience of working with controversial issues related to Northern Ireland;
- Discuss collectively with colleagues how prejudice and sectarianism might be challenged within the context of the school (and how the support of parents might be achieved).

Decisions on these issues [...] require professional judgment and review ... which takes account of:

- Appropriate activities for different age groups;
- The extent of 'progression' towards 'more difficult issues';
- Local sensitivities and shifts in current events. (Smith & Robinson, 1996, p. 31-32)

The 1996 evaluation report noted that, due to lack of a clear curriculum structure, teaching/learning materials and in-service teacher training, the outcome of the EMU initiative was unsatisfactory. 'The overall picture from pupils was of *a fragmented experience with little evidence to suggest that they perceived a coherent agenda from the themes*'; and the less able students appeared to be those who had the greatest difficulty in piecing together the fragments (Smith & Robinson, 1996, p. 25; emphasis added).

By 1998/1999 the school inspectors found that the teaching of EMU and Cultural Heritage was more satisfactory. A survey at post-primary level, however, showed that only a minority of schools had clearly defined EMU strategies within one or more subject departments, while only a small proportion of schools had developed an agreed and consistent approach to EMU objectives across all areas of study. In a majority of schools, management arrangements for policy making and planning for EMU were categorized as poor or very poor. Resources were still a problem, with a number of teachers reporting the need for accessible materials on conflict resolution (Department of Education, 2000). There is a consensus that the EMU programme has had limited impact, although it facilitated the development of excellent programmes in some schools led by innovative and enthusiastic principals. These findings indicate the limitations of a 'cross-cutting' or 'integrated' approach.

<u>Citizenship education</u>. The new citizenship programme was designed to avoid some of the problems noted with EMU. Early results suggest a positive impact. An internal evaluation of the SCPE (now Citizenship) Project found that students were 'very positive', 'thoroughly enjoyed' the classes, and had spent many hours working on letters, journals, 'Bills of Rights' and posters, which were kept in their personal portfolios.

The evaluator found that teachers had used active learning approaches, though some found SCPE 'mentally and physically exhausting'. They stated that there were plentiful resources but that these needed to be organized for each teaching module and unit. *Specific lesson plans with associated resources* would be needed if SCPE were to become part of every school curriculum, taught by teachers with varying degrees of commitment (Heaslip, 2000, p. 5, 8).

---

**Value change through discussion of diversity and rights**

Pupils thought it was important to discuss controversial issues and some indicated that their own opinions and values had been challenged in the course of debate. It was clear that some had been challenged to the point of modifying or changing their own ideas. Some pupils were concerned that there were others in their year whose ideas were too deeply entrenched to be challenged by SCPE. (Heaslip, 2000, p. 6)

---

An external evaluation found that teachers valued the attention to structure. 'It is clear that *the feature of the project most appreciated by respondents has been the SCPE framework itself, [...] the structure for activities within schools'* (emphasis added), together with flexibility and good resource materials (Watling, 2001).

A further evaluation study examined the problems of introducing citizenship into the already full curriculum, and noted that *'The one approach to implementation that elicited OVERWHELMING REJECTION was that of cross-curricularity* as represented by the current Cross Curricular Themes' (emphasis added). An element of cross-curricularity was seen as useful as a complement to the teaching of citizenship as a separate subject or discrete modules within an area of study (Birthistle, 2001, p. 4). It was considered important that citizenship be *named as the subject of study* rather than merged into other subjects; 'Pupils should be aware that what they are doing is citizenship'(Birthistle, 2001, p. 8).

These lessons learned are of great interest, since teachers in Northern Ireland are well-trained and relatively well-resourced by world standards, and still need training and support. Moreover, these well-trained teachers reject the cross-curricular or integrated approach, and favour separate and special modules clearly labelled as citizenship education. We return to these issues in Chapter V.

---

**Skills development through interactive citizenship education**

While SCPE was seen to contribute to literacy and numeracy, it was in the area of thinking and social skills that its greatest strength lay. Many people emphasized the important contribution citizenship education was making [...] to the development of thinking skills, communication, co-operation and general relationship-building skills (Birthistle, 2001, p. 9).

---

Mike Arlow[36] concluded that the most successful SCPE programmes had the following characteristics:

- Strong focus on active and experiential learning approaches;
- Discrete provision of about 5% of curriculum time;
- Classes long enough (at least an hour) to permit active pedagogies and discussion of sensitive issues;
- Specialist training for teachers and school co-ordinators for citizenship;
- Citizenship teachers and co-ordinators selected on a voluntary basis linked to personal commitment and openness to discussion of controversial issues;
- Whole school support and reflection of citizenship in subject teachers;
- Effective school;
- Staff and students awareness of human rights principles;
- Supportive senior management (Arlow, 2003, p. 30).

*Dissemination and sustainability.* Although the 1996 evaluation report was tactfully worded, it showed that there was difficulty in moving from the initiatives led by highly committed NGOs and teachers during the 1980s to universal EMU in the 1990s. One problem was the cross-curricular model, which assumed that teachers would be both motivated and able to integrate EMU into their teaching of normal school subjects, without much additional training. Even with teachers accustomed to interactive pedagogy, class discussion and democratic group decision-making, using the 'cross-cutting' or 'integrated' approach based on a curriculum decree was *not* an effective option.

Education for Mutual Understanding has continued to feature as a compulsory cross-curricular element in the school curriculum, with some improvement in implementation over the decade since it was made a statutory requirement. However, the problems of coherence and progression in student learning will remain. EMU has 'taken off' best in those particular schools where principal and governors were supportive and ensured a whole school approach. At secondary level, the impetus has now shifted to 'citizenship education', which reflects similar objectives.

Learning from the experience with EMU, the new Local and Global Citizenship programme is being introduced on a phased basis and with relatively high investment in teacher training. It is expected that seventy post-primary schools will join the programme each year from September 2002 until all schools have been absorbed. Up to five teachers from each school will receive seven days of in-service training over three years, including a residential period. There will be regular teacher surveys to explore their understanding of the concepts and their reactions to the programme (Arlow, 2003).

Initially it was expected that citizenship would become a separate subject. However, the process of consultation has left this uncertain at the time of writing. The alternative of clearly identified citizenship modules in other subjects, notably history and geography, is also under consideration, while another possibility is to leave this choice to individual schools (Arlow, 2003).

Dissemination and sustainability have been helped by the active interest of the University of Ulster School of Education in education for pluralism, social justice, democracy, human rights and the teaching of controversial issues (Arlow, 2001), including action research, evaluation exercises and interaction with the wider international community in these fields. Its degree courses in Peace and Conflict Studies at undergraduate (since 1985) and postgraduate (since 1987) levels have helped build expertise and support among serving teachers and educationalists (Duffy, 2000, p. 21). *Such involvement of national faculty in innovative programmes of the type under discussion here should be encouraged as an integral part of programme design* (see recommendations in Chapter VI below).

---

| Case study 9: Global Education |
| --- |

*Origins.* The term 'Global Education' has been used by David Selby and Graham Pike to describe their approach to curriculum renewal, developed at the University of York in England and subsequently at the International Institute for Global Education at the University of Toronto in Canada. Their monograph *Global teacher, global learner* (Pike and Selby, 1988) sets out the conceptual framework, which focuses on:

- The spatial dimension, with an emphasis on global and local interdependence;
- The temporal dimension, with an emphasis on students' roles in building a better future;

- The issues dimension, focused on development, environment, peace and human rights, emphasizing multiple perspectives and connectedness;
- The inner dimension, notably development of self-awareness and respect for others.

Beginning in 1992, Selby and Pike worked with Frank Dall, then Director of UNICEF's Middle East and North Africa (MENA) Regional Office, to support the development of global education programmes in several Arab countries, and later including Albania. The start-up of the programme in Jordan and Lebanon is described in an evaluation report by Pike and Selby (undated), and evaluation data are also available for Albania (Ashton, 2000).

*Rationale and goals.* The UNICEF initiative had the goal of helping States modernize their curricula and textbooks, which followed the traditional knowledge transmission approach. The new programme would reflect global issues and promote the development of students' self-awareness, respect and concern for others, as well as introducing interactive pedagogy. The strategy was to build a core group of interested national stakeholders and actors, followed by pilot projects in a limited number of schools, and hopefully the absorption of the best elements of the pilot project into the national curriculum and textbooks (Frank Dall, personal communication).

*Teaching/learning model.* The programme began in Jordan, with a three-day orientation workshop for national curriculum specialists, teacher educators and teachers. A core team was identified and worked with the international consultants to develop pilot materials and train the teachers who would trial them.

Phase One entailed the preparation, for grades five and six, of forty-eight model Global Education lessons: eleven in mathematics, fifteen in science, thirteen in social studies, nine in vocational education. The materials were trialled between February and April 1994 by sixteen teachers in four schools. On average each teacher attempted eight activities during the testing period. The same procedure of developing and trialling model lessons for use in the teaching of core subjects was used in later phases [37] and in other participating countries.

---

**Criteria for the development of Global Education activities**

A Global Education activity should:

- Deal with at least one of the global education dimensions of place, time, issues and individuality;
- Provide opportunities for the pupils to participate and interact with one another in pairs or small groups, and to discuss and explore together in a framework of free expression and open communication;
- Stimulate and challenge pupils to help them recall their experiences, knowledge, skills and understanding;
- Challenge the pupils by stimulating their thinking and their ability to find and develop creative solutions to problems;
- Provide organized, graduated exercises in accordance with a series of consecutive steps;
- Be suitable for pupils' developmental levels;
- Be linked to real-life situations pupils have experienced and utilize the knowledge gained from understanding contexts of social life that develop global education.[38]

---

Regarding content, the examples of lessons developed by the consultants and project staff given in the evaluation monograph focus mainly on co-operation and discussion. They used small-group and pair work, which were unfamiliar to most of the teachers. Thus, much of the challenge in starting up the programme was the introduction of participatory and interactive classroom methods. It is not clear from the examples given whether or not there was formal analysis of the sequence and overall coherence of the lessons provided to the students in the various subjects and in successive years. The model lessons developed by the programme were taught as substitutes for some of the normal lessons in the subjects concerned.

---

**Sample lessons from the Global Education programme**

*Arabic language*
- Group work with rights and responsibilities cards
- Role-plays on conflicting rights and assertiveness
- Group co-operation on non-verbal communication
- Group co-operation and negotiation on sequencing of picture cards (including example about friendship and persecution)

*Mathematics*
- Non-verbal co-operation in various mathematical activities (often using self-

---

adhesive labels with numbers on, attached to forehead or back, so that students needed to co-operate since they could not read the labels themselves)

*Science*
- Message match: students each have part of a scientific statement
- Set match: miming of animals, and linking to correct zoological group
- Paired discussion on life situation of pictured animals (caged, free)

*Social studies*
- Completion of 'bingo' card by asking about students' connections with other places
- Paired work on timelines, linking past to preferred and probable futures
- Paired ranking of statements
- Class courts. (Source: Pike & Selby, undated)

*Impact on classroom practice, teacher and student competencies and values.* Most of the teachers and principals reported their enthusiasm for the activities and for interactive learning and on the beneficial effect on students. About half of the teachers involved in Phase III in Jordan reported that their teaching approach had changed in some significant way, such as greater tolerance for students' opinions, encouraging greater self-discipline, and relying less on formal instruction. There was a change in the teacher's role from a supplier of information to animator. However, the international consultants noted that debriefing after class activities was not always well facilitated and was sometimes omitted, while 'some teachers were reluctant to pursue the broader attitudinal, values and conceptual potential of an activity'. This may reflect the relatively brief training provided for participating teachers (six days in the first stage, increased to twelve days thereafter). Pike and Selby (undated) comment that 'the achievement of affective goals is understated in the activity descriptions in many cases and is insufficiently pursued in some classrooms'.

The shift in methodology was seen likewise in the pilot project in Albania, where participative group work and whole class discussion were seen by evaluators to have increased to more than half the lesson time.

**TABLE 2:** *Percentage of student time spent in different types of learning activities (Albania)*

| | |
|---|---|
| Listening to teacher | 17% |
| Individual work | 26% |
| Group work | 32% |
| Whole class work | 24% |

Students appreciated the Global Education approach. Over 80% of the students in Jordan stated that they liked the activities very much. Pike and Selby (undated) note that the reasons given 'all relate to the operation of an open, democratic and co-operative working environment in the classroom'.

**TABLE 3:** *What students in Jordan (Phase III) liked most about the activities (percentage of students mentioning the aspect)*

| Aspect | Grade 4 | Grade 5 | Grade 6 |
|---|---|---|---|
| Co-operation | 36% | 77% | 57% |
| Discussion/dialogue | 37% | 35% | 41% |
| Working in groups | 23% | 31% | 28% |
| Freedom of opinion | 16% | 16% | 27% |
| Respect for opinions | 18% | 23% | 35% |
| Listening | 5% | 10% | 14% |
| Thinking | 19% | 12% | 22% |
| Teaching method/ activity method | 25% | 16% | 33% |
| Assimilation of information | 25% | 30% | 32% |

The students also considered that they had gained important skills and values, such as active participation in group and class activities, co-operation and mutual respect.

**TABLE 4:** *Areas in which students in Jordan (Phase II) felt they had gained through participation in the activities (percentage of students mentioning the benefit)*[39]

| Behaviour/attitude | Grade 4 | Grade 5 | Grade 6 |
|---|---|---|---|
| Participation/co-operation | 35% | 50% | 69% |
| Working in groups | 8% | 25% | 35% |
| Discussion/dialogue | 23% | 21% | 35% |
| Free expression of opinions | 10% | 23% | 17% |
| Acknowledging others' opinions | | 7% | |
| Respecting others' thoughts | 18% | 4% | 20% |
| Self-confidence | 6% | 7% | 26% |
| Trust in others | | 7% | 18% |
| Active listening | 5% | 15% | 22% |
| Free thinking | 19% | 24% | |
| Non-verbal communication | | 3% | |
| Problem-solving | 5% | 10% | |
| Enthusiasm and enjoyment of work | 6% | | |
| Shouldering learning responsibility | 2% | | 10% |
| Discipline | 5% | 10% | 10% |

Similar positive feedback was reported from Lebanon and Albania.[40] Albanian students reported enjoyment of the programme, learning about children's and human rights and the rule of law that protects those rights, increased understanding of and tolerance for others, helping academically weak pupils, finding better solutions to problems through collaboration, and personal responsibility for the future of their country. Teachers and principals reported that students were learning logical and critical thinking, expressing their views freely, showed enhanced self-esteem and tolerance for difference, more collaboration and better relationships. Teachers adopted more of a facilitator role, as required by the Global Education model lessons, with some 32% of time being spent on group work and 24% on class discussions (Ashton, 2000).

*Dissemination and sustainability.* The UNICEF initiative in Jordan, Lebanon, Albania and elsewhere showed the interest of Education Ministries in the reform of school curricula, to give more focus on the skills and values dimension of education. The model of an expanding pilot project matched the situation where teachers were unfamiliar with the student-centred, interactive approach to learning. Pike and Selby (undated) note the strong support received at official level and the desire to incorporate the Global Education approach into national education systems, while acknowledging the practical difficulties of scaling up.

---

**Mainstreaming Global Education**

In September 2002, the Jordan Education Council approved the mainstreaming of the Global Education Modules developed by UNICEF and the Ministry of Education into students' textbooks for grades four to seven. The discussion that took place focused on the enrichment these modules brought to the curricula, such as the issues of rights, equality, social responsibility, etc., and the varied learning techniques that were child-centred.[41]

In Lebanon, the decision was taken to apply the Global Education approach to a new integrated subject area for grades one to three, which brings together science and geography as elements in the subjects of English and Arabic.[42] The new subject area has been constructed on a thematic basis reflecting Global Education concerns appropriate to the age group: oneself and the others, the immediate environment, life necessities, myself and the environment, myself and health, time and weather, myself and the universe. The interactive methodology of Global Education is built into the textbooks and teacher guides.[43]

---

The Phase II evaluation report on the Albanian programme stressed the long-term nature of the project, which could not be looked on as a 'quick fix', given the need for a fundamental transformation of pedagogy from a teacher-directed to an interactive model. Given the weak economic base in Albania, and the 'fragility' of the Albanian education system, the evaluators noted that some form of outside financial support would be needed for a 'moderate' period of time. Ministry of Education officials supported the expansion of the Global Education model, as part of the programme for national education reform (Ashton, 2000).

---

**Case study 10: Experimental civics education in Romania**

---

*Origins.* The post-communist era in Romania required a new approach to the social sciences. One element was the introduction in 1991/92 of 'Civic Culture' as a subject for grades seven and eight, replacing 'The Constitution of the Socialist Republic of Romania'.[44] The question arose of whether the skills and values of civic life and culture would be better promoted using a more participatory classroom methodology and less knowledge-oriented curriculum than previously. As a first step towards answering this question, Dakmara Georgescu, a curriculum specialist of the Romanian Institute of Educational Sciences, developed experimental materials (student textbooks and teacher guides for Grades 7 and 8), as part of the project *Human Rights Education in Romanian Classrooms*. The materials were trialled in four experimental and four 'control classes' (1994-1996). Starting with the 1995/96 school year the experiment was extended to another 200 schools across the country.

*Rationale and goals.* Open-ended discussion, self-expression and a plurality of perspectives had not been possible under communist rule, but were seen as key features of democratic society. If these were to be modeled in classroom methodology alongside new content (such as the unfamiliar concepts of human rights and multi-party democracy), this would pose a major challenge to teachers. The goal was to encourage pluralistic and critical thinking, self-expression and dialogue in the classroom, as a tool for promoting long-term democratic transition in Romanian society (Tibbitts, 1997b).

*Teaching/learning model.* The outline of the alternative civic culture texts was modeled loosely on the Ministry curriculum, but adapted to include human rights principles as the underlying value system and to use activity-based approaches, including open discussion, small group and project work. The texts underwent a year of field testing by committed teachers, who provided written feedback. Ms Georgescu also undertook classroom observations and interviews with the pilot teachers and students (Tibbitts, 1997b).

The experimental model included:
- listing of specific attitudinal and skill-related goals for students;
- reduction in the amount of text;
- examples from other countries;
- questions that promoted critical and independent thinking and reflection;
- dialogue;
- paired and group work.

Topics included:
- human rights and the rights of the child;
- the identity of the person;
- relations of the individual with other persons or groups;
- norms and laws;
- the individual and the environment;
- basic democratic values and practices.

Students were encouraged to analyse the social and political environment and become active members of their society. To prepare for this work, teachers attended three half-week trainings focused on interactive methodologies and the teaching of citizenship and human rights, and received sustained professional support in using the new approaches.

*Impact on classroom practice, teacher and student competencies and values.* An impact study was conducted by Felisa Tibbitts during the 1994-95 and 1995-96 school years, with students who entered grade seven in 1994. Questionnaires were issued to students in the four classes who had followed the experimental curriculum, to students in four 'control' classes in the same schools, who had used the official textbooks, and to teachers. Classroom methods were observed and discussions were held with teachers and with focus groups of students.

The student questionnaire asked about the characteristics of a good citizen, before asking students to rate the importance of various citizenship characteristics and of selected human rights. Participatory learner-centred approaches in the alternative curriculum led to statistically significant gains over the two years in the intentions of 'voting in most elections' and 'trying to influence government decisions and policies', whereas there were no statistically significant gains in these categories for students in the comparison classrooms (Tibbitts, 1999). These statistically significant changes in valuing of more participatory forms of citizenship did not, however, emerge until two years into the programme. Thus 'two years and considerable teacher support was necessary for this result'.

*Dissemination and sustainability.* Outcomes of the field testing of the new educational materials and teacher training sessions were disseminated in education magazines, TV and radio talk shows, and project reports were published in national and international human rights education publications and/or presented at education conferences.

Dakmara Georgescu (personal communication) notes that 'the project raised several important conceptual and methodological issues regarding the identity of civic education as a subject and cross-cutting dimension in the new Romanian curriculum. Its proceedings and outcomes nourished fruitful public discussions on the matter. It also raised sometimes bitter controversies between partisans of a more "nationalistic/patriotic" model of civic education and partisans of a more "universalistic" model of civics teaching, based on the universal principles of human rights and a concept of complex citizenship (local, national, regional, European and global citizenship).'

Ms Georgescu and colleagues used the experience gained in the project to develop new syllabuses and new 'alternative' textbooks for civic education and civic culture. The Ministry of Education designated her as co-ordinator of the working group to develop new syllabuses of social studies and civic education/civic culture in the National Council for Curriculum (1995-1998).

At the time, a system of diverse (alternative) textbooks was being introduced, as part of a joint comprehensive education reform project of the Romanian government and the World Bank (1994-2002), and private publishing houses could also participate. The textbooks developed by Dakmara Georgescu and colleagues won Ministry of Education competitions in 1996, 1997, 1998 and 1999, and became 'official' textbooks that schools could choose to adopt, published by a Romanian firm. It is estimated that in each grade where civic education or civic culture is taught approximately one third of the students (around 100,000 per grade) use the textbooks on a regular basis (Dakmara Georgescu, personal communication).

---

**Case study 11: Escuela Nueva (EN)**

---

*Origins.* Escuela Nueva (EN) began as a grassroots initiative in 1975, to improve the quality of rural schooling in the coffee-producing region of Colombia. It was a refinement and expansion of the ideas from a UNESCO-sponsored 'Unitary Schools' project of the 1960s, in which multi-grade schools used co-operative learning, teacher guides and self-instructional materials prepared by teachers themselves. The pilot project of 150 Unitary Schools had led to a policy decision that all one-teacher schools should become 'Unitary', but many teachers did not understand the model or find it easy to prepare study materials themselves.

In the 1970s, a group of teachers in the province of Cali created standard learning guides with self-instructional activities for all the basic subjects for grades one to five. Small rural schools that used these guides, were called *Escuelas Nuevas*. By 1976, as a result of funding and support from UNICEF and USAID, together with Ministry of Education recognition, the EN programme was implemented in 500 primary schools throughout rural Colombia (Rugh & Bossert, 1998; Kline, 2000).

*Rationale and objectives.* The rationale was to improve student enrolment and retention in rural areas, where many children did not enrol or dropped out after grade one, by making schooling more relevant to rural life, and to introduce the principles of democracy to students and communities. School schedules were to be flexible, so that children who were absent from school because of agricultural activities would not have to repeat a year, as in traditional schools.

---

**Designing Escuela Nueva**

The programme started with two fundamental assumptions. The first was that innovation at the level of the child requires creative changes in the training of teachers, in administrative structures, and in relations with the community. [...] It features concrete strategies for children, teachers, administrative agents, and the community.

Second, from the outset, it was essential to develop mechanisms that are replicable, decentralized, and viable in a technical, political and financial sense. In other words, the design of the system had to include how to go to scale. In 1985 the programme was adopted as the national strategy to universalize primary education in rural Colombia. (Colbert et al., 1990)

---

*Teaching/learning model.* The EN model was developed for multi-grade schools with one to three teachers. The highly structured 'active learning' approach enables teachers to incorporate higher-level cognitive, affective and values objectives, even though they are coping with children of different ages and developmental levels. The teacher spends much of the time with the younger children, while the older children work alone or with one or two other students, using rural-oriented self-instructional materials in language, mathematics, natural sciences and social sciences. The study guides combine a core national curriculum with possibilities for regional and local adaptations made by the teachers during their training workshops.

---

**Curriculum content**

The curriculum promotes active and reflective learning, the ability to think, analyse, investigate, create, apply knowledge and improve children's self-esteem. It incorporates a flexible promotion mechanism and seeks the development of co-operation, comradeship, solidarity, civic participation and democratic attitudes.

The curriculum is socially relevant and inductive, and concrete. It provides active learning experiences for children. The package includes study guides for children, a school library with basic reference material, activity or learning centers, and the organization of a school government. The study guides follow a methodology that promotes active learning, cognitive abilities, discussion, group decision making and the development of skills that can be applied within the environment, thus making the link between the school and the community. (Colbert et al., 1990)

---

Management functions within the school are jointly carried out by teachers and students. Students learn democratic behaviour by participating in a 'student government', responsible for school cleaning, maintenance, sports, library, recreational activities, discipline and teaching/tutoring assistance. Students learn to collect information from the community and involve the community in the life of the school.

Teachers are trained as learning facilitators and to play a leadership role in the community. The basic training consists of three one-week courses, over the first year, supported by monthly meetings at *'microcentros'* with teachers from nearby schools. Teachers are supported likewise by the project field staff, who are trained to serve as resource persons rather than traditional supervisors.

*Impact on classroom practice, teacher and student competencies and values.* An evaluation was conducted in 1987, comparing 168 EN and sixty traditional schools. Students in grades three and five were tested in maths, Spanish, self-esteem, creativity and civic behaviour.[45] EN students were rated higher throughout, except for grade 5 mathematics and creativity.[46] Girls' self-esteem was equal to that of boys, which Colbert et al. (1990) suggest 'demonstrates the equalizing effect of the participatory methodology'. At community level there was found to be greater participation in adult education, agricultural extension, athletics competitions, health campaigns and community celebrations.

A similar programme introduced in Guatemala in the 1990s showed improved performance in language and mathematics in grades one and two, as well as in democratic practices (egalitarian beliefs — taking turns, interpersonal effectiveness — helping each other, and leadership/involvement — giving directions to their classmates). [47]

*Dissemination and sustainability*. EN has benefited from dedicated specialists who have supported its growth and dissemination. In 1978, one of the key innovators, Professor Mogollon, was transferred to the Ministry of Education to co-ordinate teacher training and the creation of regional support groups. Funding from the Inter-American Development Bank, the Federation of Coffee Growers and then a loan from the World Bank led to massive expansion during the 1980s, reaching a total of 17,948 schools in 1988, with a target of reaching all rural schools.[48] Vicky Colbert successively supported the movement as project co-ordinator, Vice-Minister of Education, UNICEF official and now from Volvamos a la Gente, a foundation she has established for this purpose, with the objective of restoring quality that was weakened during the period of rapid expansion and of educational decentralization in the country. The foundation is also trialling the approach in schools for marginalized urban children, post-primary grades and displaced populations.[49]

Scaling up had led to variations in the degree of implementation of the EN model between schools, due to practical problems such as teacher-training days being reduced, learning guides and library books not being delivered, and a lack of demonstration schools in new areas for new EN teachers to visit (Kline, 2000).[50]

The EN approach was piloted in ten small schools in Guatemala in 1989, expanding to 100 in 1992 and 200 in 1993, under the title of *Nueva Escuela Unitaria* (NEU) and with the specialist assistance of Professor Mogollon, who moved to rural Guatemala and helped teachers develop the educational materials. In the mid-1990s, various organizations supported the expansion of the programme in other regions, reaching a total of 283 government schools and over 1,000 privately funded NEU schools in 1998 (Kline, 2000).

The EN model has been widely cited as an example of good practice, academically and in terms of education for citizenship and human rights, and educators from many countries have made study visits to learn from the programme. Important lessons learned include the possibility of achieving attitudinal goals through using relatively less educated teachers, provided with guidebooks, modeling, training and support. On the other hand, the EN experience shows the problems of rapid scaling up to national level without adequate resources, even when the model has been well developed and is accepted at policy level.

| Case material: Experiences with HIV/AIDS education |
| --- |

Reference has already been made in Chapter III to some of the international experience regarding HIV/AIDS education. It is not easy to find programmes outside the Western world for which evaluation studies are in the public domain.[51] In this section, a brief overview is presented, rather than an individual case study.

A key resource is the UNICEF evaluation of national HIV/AIDS education programmes for schools in Eastern and Southern Africa conducted by Debbie Gachuhi (1999). She found that teachers were reluctant to discuss sensitive sexual topics and lacked the skills and self-confidence to use role-play for student practice in saying 'No' to unwanted or unprotected sex. Zimbabwe was commended for introducing HIV/AIDS education as a separate subject, together with infusion in relevant subjects, for all students from grade four and above. However, even there, teachers needed more training and support and were embarrassed to handle sexual topics, especially through experiential methods.

Gachuhi cites a one-year pilot project in Uganda using a control group of schools for comparison, which found that there was no impact of the pilot 'Life-Skills' curriculum and materials. Reasons for this failure were identified as:

- Teachers were not confident with experiential learning activities and reverted to conventional teaching
- Sensitive topics such as sex and condoms were avoided for religious reasons or concern over job security
- Life-Skills was non-examinable and un-timetabled. It was perceived as unimportant and many life-skills lessons not taught. (Gachuhi, 1999, p.17).

In Lesotho, Gachuhi reported that life-skills had been included in various subjects, but the curriculum was heavily biased towards knowledge, with little time or content devoted to skills and attitudes for behaviour development and change. Teachers stated that they lacked the confidence to tackle such sensitive topics. Similar limitations were noted for 'life-skills' programmes in Malawi, where there was a 'lack of appropriate teaching and learning methodologies for effectively learning skills related to safe behaviour', and in Botswana.

---

**Botswana Life-Skills Programme, 1999**

The Ministry has infused life-skills across the curriculum in secondary school subjects, such as Development Studies, Biology, Religious Education, Integrated Science, Social Studies and especially focusing on the Guidance and Counselling programme to work on skill development. Nevertheless, AIDS education is presented as one-off lessons, taught as biomedical facts to be learned for a test by teachers who are uncomfortable discussing the topic. Teachers lack participatory methods to ensure effective learning and there is little understanding of the important role life-skills play in the development of young people. (Gachuhi, 1999, p. 19)

---

Gachuhi concluded from her study that:

- Stand-alone life-skills programmes or having one lesson a week entirely separate and on its own, or a special lesson [series] within a subject like health education or biology, *have a better chance of succeeding than those that are infused in the curriculum.*
- Life-skills lessons are successful when they use participatory methods and experiential learning techniques.
- To date, there are too few life-skills programmes [...] that meet the criteria for minimally effective education programmes.
- Programmes must start early, because many young people are initiated into sex early [and also because of early drop out from school]. (Gachuhi, 1999, p. 20; emphasis in original.) [52]

Many other studies, notably in the USA, have shown similar problems with the 'infusion' approach to HIV/AIDS education, where disjointed efforts are made to convey the behavioural messages in disparate subjects. A study by the Centers for Disease Control (Kann et al., 1995, cited in Gillespie, 2002) showed that, compared to 'health educators', 'infusion teachers' were:

- less likely to be trained, and trained in fewer relevant topics;
- less likely to cover the necessary topics, especially the more sensitive and relevant topics regarding prevention;
- more likely to cover the science and biology of HIV/AIDS than preventive elements;
- less likely to include family and community elements in these programmes;
- likely to spend less time on the subject;
- less likely to use recommended resources;
- likely to use fewer interactive practices and practice of skills.

UNICEF has concluded that using specially trained teachers with a defined timetable spot for Life-Skills education is the only modality likely to impact student behaviours (Gillespie, 2002; UNICEF, 2003). Similar conclusions have been reached by the World Bank (2003, p. 383) and USAID (2002).[52]

**Answering the key questions**

In the opening chapter, we asked several questions regarding the possible contribution of education to resolving personal, social and global problems:

- Can the next generation of young people be given the skills and values to support non-violent resolution of the conflicts that confront them at personal, school and community level, linked to respect for human rights and a commitment to civic participation?
- Can education help build these skills and values in a way that will contribute to a more peaceful world, and to more just, participative and effective systems of national and international governance?
- Can education help young people learn to have respectful and non-pressured relationships that take account of the danger of sexually transmitted diseases, substance abuse and other risks to health, and minimize abusive relationships?

*Several case studies provide evidence that the answer to these questions is indeed 'Yes'.* Quantitative evaluation data from the *Reading and Writing for Critical Thinking* project, the INEE/UNHCR *Peace Education Programme*, the Lions Quest *Life-Skills* programmes, the Northern Ireland *Local and Global Citizenship* programme (or its pilot version the *Social, Civic and Political Education* project), UNICEF's *Global Education* initiatives, innovative Civic Culture education in Romania, and *Escuela Nueva* support this positive finding, as does qualitative data from most of the programmes.

The case studies make it clear, however, that positive results can only be obtained when focused efforts and resources are devoted to the initiatives. The next chapter looks at the lessons learned, in terms of programme content, methodology, placement in the curriculum and the innovation process.

NOTES

1. A pilot programme in Lebanon illustrates this point. 'A conflict-resolution project supported by the Canadian Bureau for International Education and carried out by the Lebanese Education Centre for Research and Development (ECRD) has been implemented in some Lebanese schools in the last three years. The project's main objective is to use daily problems encountered in the classroom, particularly those emerging among students, and to solve these in the classroom. Students are encouraged to overcome their problems and conflicts through dialogue, negotiation and tolerance, and not through violence: they are being trained to use language and communication, rather than physical violence, as a mode of resolving conflicts. A national team has developed resource material to be used by teachers participating in the project. Participants were trained at ECRD and monitored by a special group. An evaluation undertaken by a team of Canadian experts indicated that many teachers admitted their behaviour had changed after participation in the experience and that their students' behaviour had become significantly less aggressive.' (Frayha, 2003, p. 86)

2. There are many initiatives in education for conflict resolution and violence reduction in the 'developed countries', such as the Resolving Conflict Creatively Program developed in New York, which has resulted in a considerable reduction of school violence (ESR, 2003; Education World, 2003; Aber et al., 1998; Aber et al., 1999). These programmes, some of which cater mainly for marginalized urban youth, were not reviewed for the present study but should be included in the network building and research recommended in Chapter VI below.

3. For a summary of 'life-skills'-based health education initiatives in five Latin American countries and the Caribbean, see Mangrulkar et al. (2001, p. 38-41). Evaluations of programmes in Africa, Brazil and the USA are summarized in Whitman & Aldinger (2002, Appendix 3).

4. A 1993 Latin American survey showed that the predominant teaching method for civic education was traditional lectures which, moreover, were especially difficult for children from poorer communities to comprehend, since they related to matters outside their direct experience (Villegas-Reimers, 1994, cited in Tibbitts & Torney-Purta, 1999, p. 17).

5. The study, which included eleven post-communist nations, showed that most fourteen-year-old children understood the mechanics of democracy and expected to vote in national elections (this could be the influence of television), but many reported that they did not learn in school about the importance of voting. Some four-fifths of respondents stated that they had no expectation of getting involved in political life, such as joining a party or writing to newspapers, and only 59% thought they would collect money for a social cause (Torney-Purta et al., 2001).

6. Discovering Democracy is structured around the themes of: who rules? law and rights; the Australian nation; citizens in public life. The programme examines the role of individuals and groups in civil society and how they can contribute to change. Interesting historical and recent events were translated into classroom programmes, field-tested and adjusted on the basis of 'what works'. The final product relies heavily

on role plays, class conventions, mock television interviews, formation of mock political parties, as well as committee work to plan school and community projects. There are also student-friendly readers that broaden the coverage of the various themes. The programme is not mandatory but has the support of the States' Ministers of Education (Holt, 2001).

7.  For examples of 'life-skills', peace-education and related programmes worldwide supported by UNICEF, see 'Teachers talking' on the UNICEF website, as well as Fountain (1997).

8.  Additional leadership and direction is provided by American faculty from the University of Northern Iowa and the College of William and Mary, Virginia.

9.  A leader article in the August/September 2001 newsletter of the International Reading Association, *Reading today*, cites a total of over 30,000 educators who had participated in the programme, in twenty-eight countries, the newest being Guatemala and Pakistan (see www.readingonline.org). It mentions that there had been seventy-two external workshop leaders, drawn from the International Reading Association's American, Australian, British and Canadian membership.

10. A sister programme designed for early childhood, 'Step by Step', has also received positive evaluation for its child-centred classrooms, which cultivate decision-making, respect for others' rights, initiative and questioning (Brady et al., 1998; CRI, 2000).

11. The pedagogic model was developed in Slovakia, drawing on school change experience in the USA, as part of a USAID-funded school change initiative (Steele, 2000).

12. Some parents were reported to be concerned about the possible effects on their children's performance in national examinations.

13. This was associated statistically with teachers' incorporation of critical thinking principles into their teaching practice, and enhanced pupil/pupil interaction, rather than pupil background, teacher background or subject taught.

14. See the note on Kosovo in *Reading today*, December 2000/January 2001 issue (www.readingonline.org). See also the recent evaluation of the RWCT programme in Kosovo, which has reached 5% of Kosovar teachers. Among the interesting findings was the greater impact when training is school-based and reaches about half the teachers in a given school, rather than with conventional, non-school-based training of individual teachers (Pupovci &Taylor, 2003).

15. Peer mediation is an intervention that schools can accommodate within the framework of whole-school initiatives, given teacher interest and expertise (see, for example, Trevaskis, 1994; Dorrian, 1999; and www.mediationuk.org.uk)). This field has not been reviewed in detail for the present study, and an overview of programmes internationally and their effectiveness, as well as of manuals for schools, would be useful.

16. For a description of the programme see Baxter, 2001; Sommers, 2001; Lorenzo, 2003.

17. For details of INEE activities, see www.ineesite.org.

18. Pamela Baxter (personal communication).

19. This goal reflected the findings of the Local Capacities for Peace Project that most war-affected people are or have become moderates who would like the fighting to stop, but are unable to control the extremists whose siren calls for simplistic violent solutions had earlier led them into conflict (see Anderson, 1999).

20. Taken from the *Community workshop manual* for youth and adults (INEE, 2002). A similar sequence is used for each year of primary school, with activities adjusted according to the age group.

21. PEP's aim is for some 20% of the total population to participate, so that the concepts can reach all families. This is based on the 'social contact' idea that each student influenced by the programme can influence ten family members or friends, and an assumption that perhaps 50% of students will successfully convey basic messages through talking about the programme. Anna Obura (2002) calculated that 30% of the population aged five and above had been reached in the Kenya camps, where all school children had participated in peace education lessons, and where 12% of people aged eighteen and above had followed the community workshop programme.

22. Where possible, follow-up workshops are held after a few months, to review participants' experiences in applying the skills and concepts learned in the community workshop, and deepen their understanding.

23. Anna Obura (2002) distinguished dramas or skits self-generated by small groups of participants to illustrate a theme or skill, and role-plays (also self-generated to a large extent) that are designed to 'shock actors into new insights' by exposing them to new experiences and having to play roles different from their normal life (e.g. men having to play subservient roles as women). She advised more emphasis on the latter type of activity.

24. These trainings, which introduce the basics of classroom management as well as child development, often lead to the PEP teacher being the best trained in the school, able to advise others on teaching methods. Obura (2002) noted, moreover, that the peace education teachers were able to conduct their classes using positive approaches to classroom management in an environment where corporal punishment by teachers is commonplace. Separate training is provided for the 'facilitators' who conduct the Community Workshops.

25. Such a tracer study is needed, examining the learning outcomes retained from specific elements of the course, as well as the overall behavioural impact.

26. This correlation does not prove a causal relationship, but some contribution could be inferred from other observations.

27. Information on this programme is taken from the website www.lions-quest.org, unless stated otherwise.

28. The programme is available primarily to teachers who are trained to use it.

29. Summary from Lions-Quest website of more than sixty research studies conducted by independent agencies and internally, and audited by Pennsylvania State University.

30. EHL methodology manual, p. 15.

31. See EHL Implementation Guide and ICRC website (www.icrc.org).

32. EHL Implementation Guide, p. 4.

33. From ICRC website (www.icrc.org)

34. The new curriculum was introduced under the 1989 Education Reform Order. The cross-cutting themes of EMU and Cultural Heritage were 'conjoined' by Statutory Order in 1992.

35. Within participating schools, however, the proportion of pupils actively engaged in the Schools Community Relations Programme was often quite low.
36. Working at that time for the Northern Ireland Council for the Curriculum, Examinations and Assessment.
37. Phase III of the Jordanian programme (1995/1996) took place in thirty-five schools, involving 150 teachers and reaching 2,032 pupils. A total of 181 model Global Education lessons had been developed for use in teaching the subjects of Islamic education, Arabic language, mathematics, science, national and social education and vocational education (Pike and Selby, undated).
38. From a paper by Omar Al-Sheikh and Mustapha Abu Al-Sheik, cited in Pike and Selby (undated).
39. Data from Pike and Selby (undated). The corresponding Phase III test using a modified instrument did not show significant benefits, but qualitative data indicated that gains continued.
40. The Albania project began in 1997. At the time of the Phase II evaluation, Global Education classes were being held in eight schools, involving eighty-eight teachers and 5,100 pupils. The modules were linked to existing curricula and textbooks and covered Albanian language, civic education, mathematics, history/geography and nature studies in grades five to seven, and included topics such as human rights, environmental health, and building for the future. More activities were incorporated in mathematics and language (taught daily) than civics education (taught once a week). Thus, civics teachers implemented only two to five activities in the school year. The lack of a standardized assessment framework in Albania gave teachers some flexibility in their interpretation of the national curriculum.
41. Staneala Beckley, personal communication.
42. According to current legislation, history and civics must have separate textbooks, and could not be included in the consolidated subject.
43. Staneala Beckley, personal communication.
44. The educational transition in Romania during the 1990s is described in Georgescu & Palade (2003). Until 1994, there was a single national textbook for each subject, including for Civic Education (Grades 3, 4) and Civic Culture (Grades 7, 8) (Dakmara Georgescu, personal communication).
45. Psacharopoulos et al. (1993) cited in Kline (2000) and Schugurensky (2002). An evaluation in 1992 by Patrick McEwan also showed improved academic performance but noted that not all schools had the full range of inputs or activities (see www.iacd.oas.org). For example, student government was noted in 58% of the schools, and had been started but did not function in another 39%. Only 67% of schools had sufficient EN texts, but 94% had a library and 96% a school-made community map.
46. The results are the more noteworthy because these students came from marginalized areas and social groups.
47. Research findings cited in Kline (2000).
48. Data from the INNODATA databank on the website of the UNESCO International Bureau of Education (www.unesco.org/ibe), and Kline (2000).

49. Personal communication, and biodata from the World Economic Forum, 2003, which Ms Colbert attended as an eminent 'social entrepreneur'.
50. Organizationally, there is a co-ordination centre for EN in the Ministry of Education, regional and department level support offices and a cadre of field 'multipliers' or promoters of the EN model (Rugh & Bossert, 1998).
51. Personal communication from David Clarke. For an account of problems in HIV/AIDS education in South Africa, seen from the teachers' viewpoint, see Mannah (2002).
52. With the experiential approach, new behaviours can be modeled and then practised through role plays among small groups of students, e.g. to resist peer pressure for unsafe sexual behaviours; practising how to say 'No' to an invitation to the disco, likely to lead to drink and unprotected sex; through rehearsing responses such as wanting to be accompanied by a friend of the same sex, or the importance of completing school (WHO & UNESCO, 1994). This is difficult for 'staid', 'respectable' middle-aged teachers to organize, unless they have had a very good induction into life-skills education, which should also equip them to negotiate the content of course activities with parents and community opinion leaders.

# CHAPTER V
# Lessons learned

We have now reviewed the efforts of many educators worldwide, their achievements and the difficulties they encountered. We can celebrate their successes and try to learn from their problems.

In this chapter we shall first revisit the question of the different goals highlighted by educators and how they relate to one another. We shall review the overlap in educational objectives between the case studies, noting that rather similar approaches were needed to achieve their various goals. The implication for policy makers is that *a comprehensive approach to 'life-skills' education for peace, respect for human rights, active citizenship and preventive health is needed, which can accommodate the various goals without requiring separate initiatives for each.*

We shall next review the teaching/learning process. The lesson emerges from several of the case studies that *earmarked time is needed for behavioural skills and values development activities to have an impact,* and this time is more likely to be allocated within a comprehensive approach. Moreover, *teachers need special training* in the use of experiential approaches that deal with these sensitive topics, and this training can most practically be provided if it *covers the various goals together.* Effective programmes need *structured materials* to help teachers with this innovative work, and again it is logical to organize the materials in a *comprehensive framework* that builds reinforcement of shared skills and values as the different goals are addressed.

Thirdly, we must consider placement within the curriculum — whether to go for a separate subject approach, or whether to work through existing subjects. This is the 'hottest' issue, partly because administrators erroneously think that 'integration' or 'infusion' will avoid the need for more curriculum time. As seen in the case studies, the decision to pursue goals of peace, respect for human rights, active citizenship and preventive health through *integration as a cross-cutting issue within existing subjects is administratively easy but in many situations a recipe for failure. The separate subject approach in contrast requires courage and resources, but is rewarding for students and teachers.* The ideal approach, as will be argued below, would be a combination of *highly focused study through the separate subject approach, supplemented by attempted 'infusion'* of the same ideas in existing subjects.

A further problem in programme design is how to ensure dissemination and sustainability — scaling up. The most attractive approach cited in the case studies is the plan for introduction of Local and Global Citizenship in the secondary schools of Northern Ireland, by *expanding the network of participating schools each year,* within a policy framework that will make it compulsory, and providing extensive training and support to teachers.

The present chapter examines these issues in more detail, providing the basis for a concluding chapter on the design of a high-impact programme that can maximize education's contribution to the development of peaceful, tolerant societies with young people actively involved in community and civic affairs and enjoying healthy and unpressured relationships.

## LESSONS LEARNED REGARDING THE INTER-RELATEDNESS OF THE DIFFERENT GOALS AND OBJECTIVES

There was a high degree of overlap between the case studies in terms of themes and subject matter, and in terms of the skills, values, attitudes and behaviours sought as outcomes of the educational interventions. The norms and values of peace, tolerance, respect for diversity, non-abusive and gender-sensitive treatment of others are represented in most examples. Skills such as active listening, two-way communication, unbiased perception, appropriate assertiveness, analysis, co-operative problem-solving, negotiation and mediation recur as educational objectives in many of the case studies, though their titles differ. The Quaker Peace Education Programme in Northern Ireland attempted to bring about respect for the 'other' through peer mediation programmes based on these skills and values, which are likewise the core elements of the INEE/UNHCR Peace Education Programme. HIV/AIDS education requires a similar set of skills, applied to ways of negotiating the avoidance of unwanted or unsafe sex, as well as empathy and practical care for persons infected with the disease.

The Reading and Writing for Critical Thinking Project seeks the development of a more open and democratic society through a pedagogy focused on skills for analytical, critical and independent thinking, emphasizing the norm of respect for the views and interests of others. The new citizenship education programme in Northern Ireland is based on mutually respectful enquiry into the values of diversity and inclusion, human rights and responsibilities, equality and justice, democracy and active participation. This clearly entails communication skills, avoiding bias, polite assertiveness, co-operative problem-solving and negotiation. The experimental Civic Culture curriculum in Romania fostered the skills of pluralistic and critical thinking and the practice of dialogue, as well as appreciation of democratic values and practices and human rights.

As noted in Chapter II, there is a real problem of nomenclature — to find an umbrella title that can bring together the types of programme just discussed. Some educators feel it is essential to start from States' obligation under the Convention on the Rights of the Child to promote children's awareness of their rights and responsibilities. Based on statements in various human rights instruments and the UN Charter, some educators feel that all education in values and supporting skills should come under the umbrella of human rights education. Other educators, facing situations of ethnic distrust or post-conflict reconstruction, take the concepts of tolerance, respect for diversity, social cohesion or 'positive peace' as fundamental and see the themes of human rights as supportive. Educators faced with adolescents and youth at risk of HIV/AIDS, drug addiction or prostitution, take the view that 'life-skills' training, or 'personal and social education' for coping with the problems confronting young people, should be the focus, since these are arenas where new behavioural skills and values are needed and can be practised on a daily basis, hopefully leading to spill-over benefits for society in due course.

In this situation, educational managers can be faced with numerous proposals for enrichment and improvement of the curriculum, while their teachers state that the curriculum is already overloaded. Managers can be confused or annoyed by seemingly similar proposals coming to them under different headings such as education for peace, tolerance, human rights, rights of the child, HIV/AIDS prevention, drugs awareness, life-skills, character education, values or moral education, democracy, citizenship, etc. This type of pressure can be absorbed to some extent in rich countries with open curricula, which permit innovative teachers to develop special projects covering these topics, and where new textbooks rapidly enter the market to meet such pressures. The situation is more difficult in developing countries with under-trained teachers, minimal books or resources, and an overloaded fixed curriculum leading to knowledge-based examinations.

Inter-agency initiatives include the UN Decade for Human Rights Education (1995-2004), the Decade for Peace and Non-Violence for the Children of the World (2001-2010), and the Decade of Education for Sustainable Development (2005-2014); and UN agencies have their own initiatives in these fields. At the same time, agencies such as WHO, UNICEF and UNESCO are promoting 'life-skills' education for HIV/AIDS prevention. There are numerous specialized NGOs and networks in these areas. Many development assistance organizations support the goals under discussion here, under their various titles.[1]

It would be desirable for the professional networks supporting these various themes to initiate a process of dialogue whereby they acknowledge each others' existence and shared or overlapping goals, and seek ways of working together in the area of formal and non-formal education. Ideally, they should acknowledge that all students have the right to learn the key elements of conflict resolution, human rights, citizenship and safe personal behaviours, and find ways to co-operate in this regard and/or to incorporate these key elements in their respective programmes.

To this end, Pamela Baxter and the present author have worked together to develop an illustrative 'unified framework' for approaching the goals in Chapter II, in the context of the INEE/UNHCR approach (described in case study 3). The aim would be to provide a comprehensive and unified programme for the development of skills and values in the areas discussed in the present study. The programme, which would preferably constitute a 'separate' curriculum element, would provide the backbone for structured learning of the skills and values, which could be reinforced by learnings in other subject areas.

The model is based upon the idea that young children need to learn the basic behavioural skills and values, while children in upper primary need to consolidate these skills and values and concurrently to practise their application to their own life problems. The proposed model provides for a reversal of this process at secondary level, whereby the skills and values would be used in combination to address the most relevant issues of citizenship and adolescent life one by one. Thus, the secondary student might begin the school year with a module of four weeks on respectful peer relationships and reproductive health, and then a six-week module on human rights. Whatever the topic, these lessons would incorporate student participation in activities such as communication exercises, problem-solving, use of stories and cases, role-plays, etc., followed by interactive discussion, to help internalize the behaviours and values.

In the proposed model, knowledge objectives (e.g. on viruses and infection, civic history, or environmental pollution) remain based in normal school subjects. The one/two periods a week earmarked for skills and values under the proposed 'unified model' would nevertheless provide reinforcement of the key information and concepts, to support the role-plays and discussion.

It would be preferable (see below) for this unified curriculum component to have its own name (the 'motivational' title to be decided in discussion with students and teachers) and timetable slot. In some circumstances, however, the special programme may be included within a particular 'carrier' subject, such as civics or social studies. In this case, it is still desirable to set aside a particular period each week for the skills and values-focused work, with its own name and methodology. This period could be taught by a specialist teacher, or a teacher who is interested in entering the programme. Alternatively, the civics or social studies teachers could be provided with extensive training in methodology and content (but some of them may be unsuited to undertake this work).

*Illustrative unified model based on the Inter-Agency approach*

| Initial schooling (specific skills and values) | Middle schooling (skills and values acquisition, development and application) |
|---|---|
| Similarities and differences | Similarities and differences: *Citizenship, human rights, diversity (CHRD)* |
|  | Inclusion/exclusion: *CHRD* |
| Active listening | Active listening *Peer mediation, Gender* |
| Communication | Communication: *Sexual and reproductive health/HIV-AIDS prevention (SRH)* |
| Handling emotions | Handling emotions: *Gender, SRH* |
| Perceptions and empathy | Perceptions and empathy: *CHRD, Gender* |
| Co-operation | Co-operation: *SRH, CHRD* *Environmental conservation (EC)* |
|  | Assertiveness: *SRH, CHRD, Gender* |
|  | Analysis: *CHRD, SRH* |
| Problem-solving | Problem-solving: *SRH, CHRD, Gender, EC* |
| Conflict resolution | Conflict resolution: *SRH, CHRD, Gender, EC* |
| Negotiation | Negotiation: *SRH, CHRD, Gender, EC* |
| Mediation | Mediation: *SRH, CHRD, Gender, EC* |
| Reconciliation | Reconciliation: *SRH, CHRD, Gender* |

| Illustrative upper schooling modules (applying skills) |
| --- |

| Sexual and reproductive health/HIV/AIDS (specific themes) | Gender (specific themes) |
| --- | --- |
| ■ Communication<br>■ Handling emotions<br>■ Perceptions and empathy<br>■ Assertiveness<br>■ Negotiation | ■ Similarities and differences<br>■ Active listening<br>■ Communication<br>■ Handling emotions<br>■ Perceptions and empathy<br>■ Co-operation<br>■ Assertiveness<br>■ Analysis<br>■ Negotiation |
| **Peace, citizenship, human rights, diversity (specific themes)** | **Environment, other topics....** |
| ■ Inclusion/exclusion<br>■ Communication<br>■ Perceptions and empathy<br>■ Co-operation<br>■ Problem-solving<br>■ Conflict resolution<br>■ Negotiation<br>■ Mediation<br>■ Reconciliation | ■ Inclusion/exclusion<br>■ Communication etc., etc. |

## LESSONS LEARNED REGARDING THE TEACHING/LEARNING PROCESS

*The need for students' personal involvement in stimulus activities, skills practice and reflection*

The case studies show that competency development and personal commitment to behaviour development or change require a different pedagogy from knowledge transfer. The methodology cited by Lions-Quest is desired in most of the programmes, and is worth repeating here:

| Lions-Quest teaching/learning model |
| --- |
| The programmes are 'values-based' and provide 'sequentially designed, grade-specific classroom materials that teach competencies such as self-discipline, communication/collaboration, problem-solving, co-operation, resistance and conflict management skills. The lessons are highly interactive, and through guided skill practice, discussions and service-learning, students practice and apply the skills they are learning. |

The lesson format is often similar to that set out by the Reading and Writing for Critical Thinking programme, of 'evocation, realization of meaning and reflection'. We could describe the sequence of an effective lesson as:

1. Setting the context: remembering some of the recent learnings in this programme, the skills and concepts developed and its values.
2. 'Stimulus activity' designed to lead to new understandings, concepts and skills and/or skills practice.
3. Discussion between students, facilitated by the teacher, regarding how this fits into their future attitudes, values, view of the world and behaviour, and of any follow-up actions envisaged.

The classroom atmosphere has to be 'different', in that teachers are not telling students what to value but helping them to gain skills and insights, and internalize values, that will help them build better lives and a better society. In the Northern Ireland citizenship programme, teachers feel that students respond to this special atmosphere and open up in their discussions to include their 'real world' concerns.[2] Personal involvement of this kind requires 'labeling' of the sessions as 'special', provision of sufficient time, and special teacher preparation and support.

At the level of the curriculum framework, there needs to be a cyclic curriculum approach throughout the years of schooling that builds up skills, concepts and values over the years according to the growing child or adolescent's level of understanding, as discussed in Chapter III and illustrated by the Lions-Quest and UNHCR case studies

## THE NEED FOR DEDICATED TIME

Programmes that have made a good start in promoting the skills and values dimension of the goals cited in Chapter II feature participative, student/student interactions through practical exercises and discussion, as noted above. Successful programmes introduce new concepts, simple and complex skills, and practise or apply them repeatedly, supported by interactive discussion — personal and group reflection, which help internalize values and valued behaviour patterns.

These activities and discussions need time, what might be called 'quality time', when teacher and students exist as persons and not just as transmitters and recipients of cognitive knowledge and skills. Michael Arlow recommended an hour of specially earmarked time (see case study 8 above), so students and teachers can go deeply into the questions of a better future for their society and how to move towards it.

Pamela Baxter considers that a focused weekly lesson period throughout schooling is needed for students to develop the basic skills, values, concepts, ideas and behaviours that are supportive of peace, human rights, citizenship, gender-sensitivity and adolescent health, as in the INEE/UNHCR Peace Education Programme (see case study 3 above). In some situations, especially where a new programme is being introduced to all levels of schooling at the same time, it may be appropriate to devote an additional weekly period to the application of these skills and concepts to areas such as preventive health and adolescent relationships, especially for students in the ten-to-fourteen age range, where new 'teenage' behaviours are being developed and there is a strong risk of HIV/AIDS infection or unwanted pregnancies.

Indeed, it is almost self-evident that behavioural skill development and internalization of values will require practice and extended open discussion. Dedicated and scheduled time is needed whether a 'separate subject' approach is used or the activities are somehow inserted into one or more existing school subject. As noted below, it is difficult to find this time unless an additional period is added to the timetable or reallocated from another subject, or there is a general process of curriculum revision that reorganizes time allocations within the curriculum as a whole. It is difficult to incorporate new activities in existing subjects if their timetable allocation is not increased. In developing countries, where much lesson time is given to copying notes from the blackboard and where the syllabus is incompletely covered because copying takes too long, the problem is overwhelming. *Earmarked time* in the timetable for behavioural skills and values development is crucial.


## THE NEED FOR SPECIALLY TRAINED TEACHERS

In many countries there is still an authoritarian educational tradition, so that open-ended discussion, let alone innovative classroom activities, presents a methodological challenge to teachers. Moreover, in developing countries, teachers often lack education and professional training that would help them facilitate discussion in their classrooms or organize interactive and group activities. They have a background of 'chalk and talk' where teachers restrict what happens in the classroom to lecturing and asking closed questions (to which they know the answers), so that queries do not arise to which they cannot respond. This situation is exacerbated by a lack of reference materials.

Another difficulty is that teachers may be immersed in the culture of their own ethnic or other social group and hold unconscious prejudices or lack empathy with those who are different. They may never have thought seriously about the causes of conflict and the skills needed to minimize it. They may never have studied human rights or much of the content of citizenship. They may never have considered gender issues, or the plight of disadvantaged children. They may feel that even talking about HIV/AIDS is wrong or unbearably embarrassing. Since such matters impinge on one's daily life, one's self-image and opinions and how one fits in with those around one, teachers take time to digest and internalize new themes of this kind, ready for teaching. Ongoing periodic teacher training and support are needed, not just one-off trainings, as noted in the Exploring Humanitarian Law case study and other programmes.

A further constraint is teachers' reluctance to get into areas of public controversy, such as politics, peace agreements, ethnic differences, religious differences or sexual behaviours. The Northern Ireland experience, for example, shows that well-trained teachers, although accustomed to organizing group work and facilitating class discussion, may have difficulty in tackling politically sensitive issues, such as peace, respect for diversity and reconciliation. The implementation of Education for Mutual Understanding was held back by these factors and by the teachers' perception that they needed special training to cope with the new demands. Drawing a lesson from this experience, the new citizenship programme is being phased in slowly so that a group of teachers at each school can be well trained, will have a self-image as trained citizenship teachers and can support each other when starting up.

It is clear from the weak performance of HIV/AIDS education in Africa that many teachers are too embarrassed to tackle sexual behaviour issues even when it is a life-and-death matter for their students. Performance is better where teachers specifically trained in 'AIDS education' have a self-image and mandate from the education authorities to tackle this difficult area.

The evaluation of the UNHCR Peace Education Programme in Kenya showed that a separate cadre of teachers who were given intensive training in classroom methodology and the PEP activities could work successfully despite inadequacies in their school education and prior professional training. Here, the selection of suitable candidates, namely those with an interest in and apparent capacity to lead activity-based approaches, together with regular in-school support from programme staff and the motivation of the teachers and facilitators to keep their jobs, created a reasonably well-functioning programme and strengthened peace-oriented behaviours in the camps.

Evidently, the training cannot be quick and one-off. Trainers and then teachers have to develop and internalize new skills and values, and need extended in-service training and ongoing support, such as regular vacation courses, the use of specialist mobile trainers, the use of school clusters, etc. A good approach is to start with a first group of schools, and use them as the training models for another group, and so on — a model used by Escuela Nueva. The cascade approach, with short training courses for trainers who then give short courses for school teachers, *cannot* meet the needs of teacher development in the area of behavioural and values development and change.

The role of teacher-training colleges and of education faculties at university level will depend on local circumstances. At a minimum, workshops on peace, respect for human rights, active citizenship and 'life-skills' for preventive health should be introduced for all trainee teachers. This will build towards a future where these values can be reflected in the teaching of all subjects and in the whole school setting. Ideally, one or more teacher colleges or faculties can serve as centres for the in-service training and support of teachers specializing in this area.[3]

Over the longer term, there should be a review of the teacher education process, to make explicit the linkages and extensive overlap between the skills and behaviours discussed in this study and those included in training for classroom management and effective pedagogy.

## THE NEED FOR A 'WHOLE SCHOOL' APPROACH

The best way of learning is through example and practice. Thus, a school climate based on respect for human rights and democratic principles will reinforce the ideas taught in class. This includes the right for children to express their reasoned views, the principle of student representation, and serious attention being given to the deliberations of student councils. The development of an anti-bullying policy based on student inputs and feedback is an example of 'whole school' attention to basic human rights, and should be presented as such. The development of peer mediation mechanisms represents a major step forward in enhancing students' understanding of conflict and how it can be resolved. Co-curricular activities such as social service or cross-community activities can help reinforce the behavioural messages and concepts.

Clearly, the pedagogic methods used in the school will influence the impact of special lessons on communication, co-operation, human rights, citizenship and respectful relationships that preserve mental and physical health. Teachers' willingness to listen and involve all students (male or female) fairly in class discussions, and teachers' handling of wrong answers as a positive tool for class learning rather than an occasion to humiliate a student, will impact daily on students' personal growth.

The appointment of a school co-ordinator to multiply the efforts of teachers to reflect education for peace, citizenship, etc., in their own subject teaching and other school activities will strengthen the whole school approach, notably where the principal gives his or her support. This was a feature of schools that were more successful in addressing the challenge of implementing Education for Mutual Understanding.

## THE NEED FOR A 'WHOLE COMMUNITY' APPROACH

Children are greatly influenced by their homes and community and have difficulty registering and internalizing school-taught ideals that conflict with the reality around them. Moreover, schools have difficulty in implementing innovative programmes the community opposes. Education for Mutual Understanding in Northern Ireland was seen by some people as having political implications benefiting their opponents, and teachers were cautious due to fear of parental reactions. HIV/AIDS education in schools is often treated superficially because of teachers' fear of parental opposition.

Effective programmes must therefore begin with involvement of key stakeholders, and approaches must be adjusted through negotiations to take account of community norms[4]. There must be local ownership of the programme. A first step in the Global Education programme, for example, was to hold introductory workshops for national and local stakeholders. Non-formal education as a complement to school-based programmes can help overcome this problem. The 'community' (youth and adult) component of the INEE/UNHCR peace education programme (twelve-session 'community workshops') has proved popular in several countries, attracting community leaders, youth, teachers (other than peace education teachers) and others.

---

**The Kanun of Leke Dukagjini**

The human rights situation in Northern Albania is limited by adherence to the 'Kanun of Leke Dukagjini', a time-honoured oral code governing issues such as property rights, marriage and inheritance. In particular, it specifies that the killing of a family member must be followed by a revenge killing, carried out by a relative. This code still creates problems for families entangled in blood feuds. A concerted effort is being made to gradually change this culture and build respect for human rights, modern law and good citizenship, through a 'whole community approach', using workshops, discussion groups, drama, magazines and training of school teachers, led by international and local NGOs, churches and other civil society groups, as well as governmental agencies.[5]

---

In this regard, the role of NGOs is especially important, particularly for non-formal education of adults.[6] NGOs are subject to fewer bureaucratic pressures and delays, and can adjust to the particularities of local situations, so it is important to help them build capacity in this area.

## ASSESSMENT

Assessment of achievement is widely believed by teachers to be important for motivating students. It does not feature strongly in the literature reviewed for this study, partly because of the innovative nature of the programmes, and partly because of the importance of non-cognitive objectives, for which normal approaches to assessment are inappropriate. The matter has been discussed recently in connection with citizenship education — it is considered undesirable to give anyone poor marks as a future citizen on the basis that he or she is not very good at writing examination papers. A range of assessment measures for individual and group work is suggested for the new citizenship programme in the UK: for example, planning and delivering a talk or presentation, producing a diary, logbook or portfolio of citizenship education activities, involvement in class, school, community and environmental discussions, role-plays, activities and councils and so on.[7]

## RESEARCH, MONITORING AND EVALUATION

Given the sensitive nature of values and behavioural norms, it is especially important to begin programmes of the type considered here with participatory research, in which the existing feelings and viewpoints of the 'target groups', their likely teachers and the wider community are elicited. [8] In the start-up of the UNHCR peace education programme, the consultant held eighty meetings with numerous groups and individuals in the refugee camps in Northern and Eastern Kenya, as a first step in developing the programme. This led on to programme development in close liaison with the refugee teachers. Thus it was that at a later stage, one of the adults attending a peace education workshop commented that:

> Whoever designed this programme understands us very well. This allows us to discuss all that is important in our lives and understand that everything we do is important (for peace). [9]

It is likewise important at the stage of programme design to think ahead to monitoring and formative evaluation activities, and undertake a baseline study.

130

Formative evaluation should look at activities actually undertaken, teaching/learning processes and at the learnings resulting from the various elements in the course, so that there can be continuing improvement in the programme's effectiveness .[10]

Given the many problems that occur in such new programmes, it is crucial to undertake continuing monitoring of implementation as well as formative evaluation and research on the experience, learning and perspectives of participants (students, teachers) and the wider community. Intensive evaluation is expected to accompany the compulsory though phased introduction of citizenship in Northern Ireland. The evaluation should include follow up of ex-students.[11]

## LESSONS LEARNED REGARDING SEPARATENESS OR INTEGRATION/INFUSION OF PEACE, CITIZENSHIP, HUMAN RIGHTS AND PREVENTIVE HEALTH INTERVENTIONS IN THE CURRICULUM

The biggest controversy in the field under discussion concerns the separateness or otherwise of the intervention in the curriculum. Many teachers feel the timetable is already overcrowded and resist giving up a weekly period to cover education for peace, active citizenship, relationship education or whatever title is used. Teachers argue that the classes they already teach provide the skills and values needed to achieve the goals in Chapter II. However, the experience with 'cross-cutting issues' cited in the Northern Ireland case study shows that the result is patchy at best, with students' experience of the issue being fragmented and lacking coherence and progression.

Administrators argue that 'integration' in one or more existing subjects will avoid the need for a special period devoted to 'life-skills', 'citizenship' or other goals. However, let us be clear that this argument is not valid. We are talking about an additional participative period of work each week. *It will take time from existing activities under any arrangement other than the addition of an extra period to the timetable.*[12]

It is true that for early primary school grades, if there is a *flexible* curriculum, and if teachers have the needed skills and commitment, 'integration' of special lesson units may be possible. The same is true for non-formal education. But for older students, if there are to be participative exercises followed by reflection, as in most of the activities reviewed in this study, then a *40-60 minute weekly special session is needed, whether treated as a separate subject or a special 'practical' unit within another subject.*

Given these findings from the study, let us examine the debate regarding the separate subject issue. We are looking at the process of introducing focused interventions to build skills and values needed for the goals of peace and conflict resolution, respect for human rights, active citizenship, healthy relationships and health-preserving behaviours. The models of intervention have been variously classified by different actors. Gillespie (2002), writing about skills-based health education, distinguishes:

- 'integration/infusion' alone (the skills and values are included in all or many existing subjects and taught by regular classroom teachers)
- the 'carrier subject' approach (the theme is included in a single subject such as social studies, biology or health education, and typically would be taught by the concerned teacher)
- the 'separate subject' approach (the theme is taught as a specific subject, by identified and specially trained teachers) (this is found to be the most effective).

Pamela Baxter (personal communication) uses the term 'cross-referencing' to refer to another approach where the programme requires teachers in one or more subjects to incorporate special lesson units at suitable points in their courses. She distinguishes:

- the 'total infusion' approach, within a relatively 'open' (flexible) curriculum (all teachers)
- the 'cross-referencing' approach (project staff prepare lesson units for insertion at various points in the teaching of certain subjects)
- the 'separate subject' approach (peace education or some other motivational theme appears on the school timetable, and may have separate teachers).

The experience reviewed in this study shows major problems with the 'integrative' approach. As noted earlier, the Northern Ireland decision to introduce Education for Mutual Understanding as a cross-cutting issue for all subjects led to fragmentation and lack of cohesion in the educational experience of the students, since different teachers worked in relative isolation to incorporate this dimension into their programmes. Teachers were adamant that the new citizenship programme should *not* be a cross-cutting theme.

The cross-referencing approach does not solve the problem. The Global Education pilot projects showed the considerable resources that were needed to insert even a few lessons on 'global' principles into the teaching of regular subjects. UNESCO-PEER and UNHCR invested considerable resources in an initiative to raise environmental awareness and responsibility in refugee schools in East Africa, using a 'cross-referencing' model. Workbooks and teacher guides for each school grade from one to eight focused on activity-based approaches to environmental conservation and sustainability. But hard-pressed subject teachers focused on preparing their students for examinations had difficulty in using the cross-referencing system and had little incentive to do so.

---

**UNESCO-PEER/UNHCR Environmental Education Programme in East Africa**

UNESCO's Programme for Education in Emergencies and Reconstruction (PEER), with support from UNHCR, initiated the production of environmental educational materials to raise awareness of positive environmental behaviours among students in refugee schools in several East African countries. The materials were for the production of experiential lesson units that could be inserted into the teaching of science and social studies lessons through a cross-referencing approach (Talbot & Muigai, 1998). Although attractive materials were produced the impact was limited. Lessons learned included:

- The cross-referencing approach is too complex and overburdened teachers did not have time or incentives to insert this additional material into their plan of work.
- Local production of experiential materials by local professionals not well inducted into activity-based and interactive approaches was problematic.[13]

---

As noted earlier, experience with HIV/AIDS education in the USA indicates the need for clear and explicit modeling and focus on the relationship skills and values to be conveyed, which even in that country is difficult as part of regular science or social studies lessons. Gachuhi's review of HIV/AIDS education in Eastern and Southern Africa likewise showed the failure of regular teachers to tackle sensitive issues relating to sexual behaviour, even when this was government policy.[14] She recommended a 'carrier subject' approach, with health education teachers being trained to incorporate specific HIV/AIDS education modules in the health education curriculum.

In the carrier-subject approach, the teachers of a particular school subject (e.g. civics, science, health or mother tongue) are specially trained to deliver the programme, and deliver it as a separate labelled 'practical' component with its own weekly slot. The carrier-subject approach has the disadvantage that teachers cannot be selected for their personal qualities. A middle-aged or elderly disciplinarian, a modest young woman or nun may have difficulty facilitating participative discussions among adolescents and youth, especially on sexual matters. Another very important disadvantage is that examination pressure may lead to the quiet utilization of the 'experiential' time slot for note-taking and examination-cramming activities in other aspects of the 'carrier' subject.

The evaluation of the UNHCR Peace Education Programme in Kenya showed that the 'separate subject' approach, with a separate cadre of teachers who were given intensive training in classroom methodology and the PEP activities, could work successfully and strengthen peace-oriented behaviours in the camps. The Norwegian Refugee Council programme in the Caucasus did not use separate teachers, but teachers trained under the programme mostly gave their human rights lessons as a separate subject, in an additional school period added on to the normal weekly timetable.

The ideal is thus a 'separate subject' timetabled period for which suitable teachers can be selected and trained to facilitate experiential work. It may seem that the separate subject approach (or a properly organized carrier-subject approach) with extensive training of specially identified teachers is a high-cost model. However, this approach can be cost-effective. Most teachers, especially in developing countries, need extensive and continuing in-service training to gain understanding of and effectiveness in teaching skills for conflict resolution and tolerance of social diversity, human rights, active citizenship or adolescent sexual safety. It thus helps to have a limited number of teachers to train and support, and for them to be practising the teaching of these subjects as the major part of their work.[15, 16]

'Explicit' and 'officially timetabled' approaches of the 'separate subject' type or modifications of it are widely recommended, based on the failure of 'infusion' and 'integration' approaches (Weare & Gray, 2003; World Bank, 2003; Gachuhi, 1999; Gillespie, 2002; Elias, 2003; Arlow, 2003).

In deciding upon a strategy it is well to remember the 'stages' model developed by Clarence Beeby, who believed that flexibility to be creative in the classroom reflected the teachers' general level of education and training. Only highly trained teachers have the flexibility and educational background to successfully implement the 'integration/infusion' approach, even with younger children.

We now know, from initiatives such as the Bangladesh Rural Advancement Committee's extensive school system, as well as from programmes discussed in this study, that with intensive training and support it is possible for teachers with modest education to teach for meaning and for peace and citizenship. However, it is important to remember that Education for Mutual Understanding in Northern Ireland, a country whose education system is at Beeby's stage four, ran into major difficulties because it was assumed that the teachers could easily integrate new elements into their regular teaching. If such integration is difficult for teachers at level four, one must be very careful about assuming that is possible for levels one to three.

## *Comparison of intervention models for behavioural skills and values development*

| | Advantages | Typical problems |
|---|---|---|
| Integration/ infusion approaches | ● A 'whole school' approach<br>● Uses accepted school subjects<br>● Many teachers involved<br>● Potential for reinforcement | ● Difficulty of ensuring cohesion and progression in what students learn (skills and values for peace, human rights, citizenship, preventive health behaviours)<br>● Difficulty of accessing, training and supporting all teachers in skills-based experiential approaches and influencing all textbooks<br>● Bias to information transmission in content and methodology (same as for other subjects)<br>● Lack of lesson time for experiential activities and discussion<br>● Can be lost among higher status elements of currriculum<br>● Pressure to focus on examination topics<br>● Some teachers do not see relevance to their subject<br>● Potential for reinforcement seldom realized due to other barriers<br>● Teacher turnover necessitates long-term training and support programmes |
| Cross-referencing approaches | ● Special skills and values-focused lesson units prepared centrally for insertion by subject teachers as enrichment or application of certain topics means that information and guidance is provided to non-specialist teachers | ● Difficulty of cross-referencing to subject syllabi<br>● Difficulty of accessing, training and supporting teachers of subjects concerned in skills-based approaches<br>● Lack of lesson time for experiential activities and discussion<br>● Pressure to focus on examination topics<br>● Teacher turnover necessitates long-term training and support programmes |
| Carrier-subject approaches | ● Teacher training and support easier because fewer teachers involved and some have relevant background due to their subject experience<br>● Teachers more likely to see the relevance of the skills and values<br>● Cheaper and faster to integrate the components into materials of one subject than to infuse them across all | ● Risk of an inappropriate subject being chosen (e.g. biology is less good than health education or civic education for HIV/AIDS education because of the social and personal issues, and the tendency of science teachers to focus only on transmission of knowledge)<br>● Needs an extra timetable period for new experiential content<br>● Pressure to focus on examination topics<br>● Some of the subject teachers may be unsuited to experiential approaches and facilitating discussion of sensitive topics<br>● Teacher turnover necessitates long-term training and support programmes |
| Separate subject approaches | ● The specially trained teacher needs intensive training but through constant practice gains competence and is motivated to keep the job by actually teaching the skills, values and behaviours required by his employers<br>● Clear labelling of the subject and adequate time allocation assist students to internalize appropriate values and behaviours | ● Requires decision to find space in existing timetable or add an additional school period to the school week<br>● Pressures on the specially trained teachers to do other things, especially if their programme is given low status<br>● In small isolated schools, the specialist teachers need additional tasks to fill their timetable<br>● Teacher turnover necessitates long-term training and support programmes |

*Adapted from Gillespie (2002) and Baxter (personal communication).*

---

**Beeby's stages in the growth of a primary school system**

1. *Dame school:* teachers poorly educated, untrained: narrow subject content, memorizing very important
2. *Formalism:* teachers poorly educated, poorly trained: rigid curriculum, memorizing and external exams important, emotional life largely ignored
3. *Transition:* teachers better educated, better trained: more emphasis on meaning but teachers hesitate to use greater freedom, examinations restrict experimentation, emotional and creative dimension limited.
4. *Meaning:* teachers well-educated, well-trained: meaning and understanding stressed, variety of content and methods, positive discipline, emotional and aesthetic dimensions, closer relation with community — better buildings and equipment essential (Beeby, 1966, p. 72, cited in Renwick, 1998)

---

'Integration' should be easier in non-formal education, since there are fewer pressures from external examinations or parents. However, the problem of teaching capacity is still a major hurdle. A survey of 'life-skills' education by NGOs in India concluded that success:

> will depend on giving it a fully worked out curriculum, teaching learning materials, training and links with the formal system. [...] The goal should be to prepare a kit, a curriculum to integrate life-skills, a training package to promulgate learner friendly methodology and life-skills integrated teaching/learning materials that are multi-sensory. [...] Unless the new approach of life-skills is spelled out with concrete teaching learning materials it remains incomprehensible to the volunteer worker or facilitators and even to the social worker in NGO set ups. They are familiar with the message but not trained in teaching/learning transaction. [...] There should be support from print media, radio and television. (Remedia Trust, undated)

# LESSONS LEARNED REGARDING THE PROCESS OF INNOVATION

*Adoption of innovations*

Studies of planned organizational change have identified different ways of convincing staff to participate. An early formulation by Chin and Benne (1969) distinguished power-coercive, normative-re-educative and rational-empirical strategies, with normative-re-educative often being the most effective. The 'power-coercive' approach was used in Northern Ireland, where *Education for Mutual Understanding* was introduced through an Education Order but with limited success. This authority-based approach is ineffective when complex changes in human behaviour are required. The 'rational-empirical' arguments in favour of EMU were insufficiently persuasive for many teachers to develop new activities in a field they considered difficult. Moreover, there was limited 'normative-re-educative' support through teacher training, and many staff did not internalize the norm of integrating EMU into their activities. The new *citizenship* programme for Northern Ireland secondary schools, in contrast, is being introduced with a strong 'normative-re-educative' basis, through extensive teacher training and the use of pilot schools to demonstrate the feasibility and rationality of the reform. In this setting, compulsion provides additional motivation for schools to take the matter seriously, rather than being a stand-alone intervention.

Relevant here are the personal characteristics identified by Everett Rogers (1995) in relation to the diffusion of innovations. A few people are natural *innovators*, and a few are interested to keep up with the new — *early adopters*. An estimated 30% are *early majority adopters*, who follow the trend quite willingly, while another 30% are *late majority adopters*, who decide they should follow the others for economic reasons, to keep their job, etc. Last come the *laggards*, who constitute the Achilles heel in respect of educational innovations, since their poor performance can undermine the programme as a whole.[17] At the level of schools, Slavin (1998) suggests that there are a *few seed schools* where innovation can easily germinate, that have 'an extraordinary capacity to translate a vision into reality', and a majority of *brick schools*, which need 'bricks' — structured teachers' materials, student materials and other supports to 'build' change, together with a few *sand schools*, where change is difficult.[18]

Naturally innovative teachers and 'seed schools' can be empowered by a new policy and its rationale to innovate creatively, and 'early adopter' teachers will be keen to follow in their footsteps. But a 'normative-re-educative' process is required to get others on board, together with the 'bricks' of supporting teaching/learning materials. Hence, the emphasis throughout this study on the need for specially trained teachers and their long-term support as well as structured educational materials – features characteristic of several of the programmes described in Chapter II. Close contact with change agents, through training and support, is required, using inter-personal forms of communication, helping identify needs and solve problems (Hood, 1982, cited in Hord, 1992). The Rand Change Agent Study conceptualized the stages of the change process in schools as initiation, implementation and incorporation or ownership. Success was characterized by:

- planning for adapting the change to the local setting;
- teacher participation in adapting materials to the needs of the school;
- teacher training that was concrete, specific and ongoing;
- classroom consultation and advice from resource personnel;
- modeling by more experienced teachers;
- a critical mass of innovating teachers;
- active support of the principal (Berman & McLaughlin, 1978, cited in Hord, 1992).[19]

The critical element in educational innovation is staff development, which requires not just training workshops but on-the-job support in the workplace. Joyce and Showers (1980) summarized best practice in staff development as presentation of theory, demonstration, practice under simulated conditions to ensure 'fluid' control of the new skills, followed by regular on-site coaching and preparing teachers to provide one another with coaching.

Although these studies refer to the US and Europe, there is little doubt that they apply elsewhere.[20, 21] A review of the problems encountered by developing countries that introduced innovative pre-vocational and work-experience programmes as an addition to the school programme showed the failure of attempts to introduce these unfamiliar programmes on a compulsory basis, without a 'normative-re-educative' approach (Sinclair, 1980). The author suggested three options, with preference given to step-wise expansion of a network of participating schools, with strong government support.[22]

The more successful of the initiatives described in Chapter IV incorporate a strong 'normative-re-educative' approach. For example, the UNHCR initiative in Kenya used a cadre of peace-education teachers selected for having the personal qualities and interests of innovators or early adopters, who were provided with substantial training, well-structured materials and ongoing technical support. The Global Education initiatives worked with a core group of forward-looking educators, and built up a network of committed pilot teachers in participating schools.

The Escuela Nueva began with a network approach, building up teacher expertise through training, including visits to functioning EN schools, and well-structured educational materials. The efforts to extend the programme rapidly to all rural schools in Colombia, together with teacher transfers, led to a dilution of teacher support and hence of the innovative features in some schools. The citizenship programme in Northern Ireland is providing intensive teacher support in the framework of a phased but compulsory scaling up. This could be a useful model for other countries.

Several programmes described in the present study avoided the problems of scaling up to national level by use of the volunteer principle, attracting many natural innovators and early adopters, as, for example, in the *Reading and Writing for Critical Thinking* teacher-training programme.

The commitment of policy makers in deeds rather than words is critical. A 1995 review of skills-based *Health and Family Life* education programmes in the Caribbean, initiated in 1981 by the Pan American Health Organisation and the University of the West Indies, supported by CARICOM,[23] found mostly an emphasis on information transfer over skills development and participatory methods.[24] Respondents indicated that Health and Family Life Education needed to be placed higher on policy-makers' agendas, so that teacher training could be strengthened and the quality of teaching materials improved (Mangrulkar et al., 2001, p. 40-41).

These experiences are in line with a World Health Organisation review of strategies for promoting skills-based health education, which suggested that where behavioural outcomes are desired, there is a need to move:

1. Away from small-scale projects; towards going to scale
2. Away from education programmes develop in isolation; towards a comprehensive approach
3. Away from attempts to infuse health topics across many subjects; towards effective placement within the curriculum
4. Away from creating new materials; towards using existing materials better
5. Away from generic life-skills programmes that are not attached to specific objectives and goals; towards linking content to behavioural objectives
6. Away from delivery by unprepared adults; towards consistent, ongoing professional development for teachers and support teams (WHO, 2003a, p. 32)

## INNOVATION AFTER POLITICAL TRANSITION

The process of innovation is more complex when a major process of educational restructuring is taking place after the fall of a previous regime, as in the reconstruction of education in Afghanistan after the fall of the Taliban in 2001, for example. In such circumstances, the decision-making process is complicated by the need to establish new management structures and build staff capacity. It is difficult at such times to initiate nation-wide programmes of the type under discussion here, although such programmes can flourish in a receptive atmosphere if initiated by NGOs or others. The experience of Eastern Europe was cited earlier, showing that time is required for innovations to be developed and disseminated.[25]

It is important to create the capacity to develop new programmes. In Romania, one of the first steps after the fall of the dictatorship was to re-open the Institute for Educational Sciences, and the faculties of education, psychology and sociology, which had been closed for political reasons (Georgescu & Palade, 2003). This led in time to the experimental civics programme described in Chapter IV. As noted in the Norwegian Refugee Council experience in the Caucasus, it is important to create 'core groups' to work with Education Ministries to pursue the human rights/citizenship agenda during a period of transition (Johannessen, 2000).

A new curriculum framework has to be developed that can empower movement towards behavioural skills, concepts and values development. As an example, the New Kosovo Curriculum Framework developed in 2001 was based on the general principles of pluralism, learner-friendliness,[26] unity and diversity, creativity, holistic and integrated learning, student orientation, as well as adjustment to modern developments, consultation and process, autonomy and accountability (Georgescu, 2001). Likewise, a new framework has been developed for civics education in Rwanda, as noted in Chapter II. Hopefully the lessons learned in the present study may be helpful in bringing these and other curriculum aspirations to fruition.

## APPROACHING OUR CONCLUSIONS

We have seen in the present study that it is possible to create education programmes supportive of the goals in Chapter II. *These programmes cannot, of course, create local or world peace or a Scandinavian-type model state or an end to risky health behaviours. Many other factors influence whether these outcomes are achieved.* Yet, over the long term, it may indeed be true that 'the pen' and ideas for peaceful, sustainable and health-promoting behaviours can be 'mightier than the sword', that working on young people's thinking and values may lead to general acceptance of important norms for local and global citizenship. Few people now publicly defend slavery or torture, but these were considered normal in ancient and medieval times. The idea that all nations should agree on basic human rights and responsibilities, that there should be universal respect for the dignity of all, is quite new, taking off in the 1940s, although building on what had gone before.

So why not work towards the concept that we should all have the skills and value orientations to resolve conflicts peacefully in our lives and in our societies, and to contribute actively to solving local and global problems as concerned citizens? That we should have a strand within our education programmes that explicitly introduces students to the practical skills, concepts and values needed for us all to live together?

If educators are to take up this challenge, they have to work with representatives of all stakeholders and locate resources for such an initiative. As shown in this chapter, the crucial concerns are:

1. *A unified framework:* putting together into *one curriculum framework* the goals and education objectives for skills and values development supportive of conflict prevention, respect for human rights, active citizenship, preventive health, including HIV/AIDS prevention, and related concerns.
2. *Special time and resources: deciding to earmark special curriculum time* (basically one period a week) for special interactive education activities aligned to these objectives, to be used by *specially trained teachers with special supporting materials and ongoing expert guidance.*
3. Separate *labelled programme identity:* Deciding to use a *'separate subject'* — or, less effectively, a *'carrier- subject,* — approach as the main thrust of the initiative with supporting 'infusion' of the educational objectives into other subjects. There would be a *cyclic curriculum* with modules focused on locally appropriate *'motivational themes'.*
4. *Expanding network approach:* Use of a fast-track pilot school approach, with *progressive expansion of the network* of participating schools and other educational institutions, including teacher education colleges and faculties.

## NOTES

1.  See, for example, the use of the ActionAid 'REFLECT' literacy model in Burundi to promote peace through inter-ethnic study groups in Burundi (Bennett, 2003). 'Conscientization' is a major theme of many NGO programmes worldwide, including those outside the education sector.
2.  Statement by Michel Arlow at International Bureau of Education seminar, March 2003.
3.  According to a recent study, the characteristics of outstanding teachers include analytical and conceptual thinking skills, relating to others (impact and influence, teamwork, understanding others), leading, planning and setting expectations, and professionalism (including creating trust, having respect for others) (McBer, 2000). There is evident overlap with the skills and values discussed in this study.
4.  Parents in some countries are reluctant to permit education that refers to sexual acts, even if the   emphasis is on the associated health dangers, fearing that it will promote promiscuity (although there is evidence to the contrary). Teachers are sometimes reluctant to show and explain diagrams of reproductive organs, for religious reasons, or because they regard certain words in the local language as 'vulgar'. Such issues have to be negotiated and compromises found in the pilot phase of innovative programmes.
5.  Nancy Drost (personal communication), based on discussions with World Vision, Canada.
6.  As noted in the case of human rights education, for example, by Lohrenscheit (2002). For a review of NGO databases on human rights education see Lebmann (2002). For an example of a planning document, see CDE (2000). For an example of non-formal training of grass roots community leaders, as well as teachers, by the Peruvian NGO Institute for Education in Human Rights and Peace, see Bernbaum (1999). It is useful to identify and involve local human rights, peace-building, environmental and citizenship NGOs in 'scoping' the framework for curriculum initiatives in this area.
7.  For a review of some of the assessment issues and possibilities in this type of work, see: www.qca.org.uk/citizenship and Kerr (2002).
8.  Participatory research on children's and teachers' perspectives on peace and reconciliation are envisaged as a first step in a new initiative of education for peace and reconciliation in Rwanda.
9.  Cited in a UNHCR booklet on the programme.
10.  See, for example, Maoz (2002).
11.  The planned eight-year UK longitudinal study of citizenship education will track a cohort of young people who entered secondary school in 2002 and will thus be the first to have a continuous entitlement to citizenship education (Kerr, 2002).
12.  The extra period was acceptable to the Kenya refugee schools because of the concern for peace.  Likewise most of the teachers in the Norwegian Refugee Council programme in schools in the Caucasus chose to add an extra period to the timetable because of their desire to teach human rights.
13.  Chris Taylor and Chris Talbot, personal communications. A case study of this programme is being undertaken by Lyndsay Bird.
14.  Evaluation of a government pilot programme for special accreditation of teachers of Sex and Relationship Education in England and Wales showed that teachers were

interested in being accredited, though suggesting a broader approach, recognizing good practice in Personal, Social and Health Education (Warwick et al., 2002).

15. All the interventions reviewed here have a quite high start-up cost because of the need for a team of local professionals to familiarize themselves with the field, to review and take decisions on materials, to train trainers, and to provide initial and ongoing in-service teacher training. After three to four years, practising 'separate subject' teachers may have acquired the key competencies, and require mainly top-up trainings and motivation/monitoring. Due to teacher turnover, there will be an ongoing need for teacher training, but much less than if all teachers have to be trained in this special area of pedagogy.

16. A recent proposal for peace and human rights education in Sierra Leone, developed for the World Bank, includes both cross-cutting 'separate subject' themes and topics cross-referenced to regular subjects (Bretherton et al., 2002). If the aim is to use the programme in all schools, the cost of in-service training and in-school support, reaching all teachers, many with weak education and professional backgrounds, would be very high.

17. Innovation characteristics are also important. Rogers describes five features with a major influence on uptake of the innovation: relative advantage, compatibility, complexity, trialability and observability. His theory was developed to explain uptake by individuals of innovations in fields such as agriculture and health, but provides a useful insight into why 'policy' and 'practice' so often diverge in public sector activities such as education.

18. Slavin estimates that in the US fewer than 5% of primary schools are in the 'seed' category, while perhaps 90% are in the 'bricks' capacity.

19. Another study found that success in school improvement programmes was associated with: 'carefully developed and well-defined curricular and instructional processes; credible training; ongoing assistance and support for teachers provided by district staff, external trainers and linkers, and other teachers; assistance and firm direction from administrators'. (Crandall, 1982, cited in Hord, 1992)

20. In a study of the Aga Khan Foundation's school improvement projects in East Africa, Hopkins (2002) notes similar issues. Regarding the barrier between in-service training and classroom implementation, he suggests the need for peer coaching teams within the school, and head-teacher participation.

21. The seminal concepts of Lewin (1936), who conceptualized the stages of change as 'unfreezing', 'change' and 'refreezing', are relevant to the transformation of teachers with their personal style of teaching, as well as the behavioural development of their students. This is why 'special' training is needed, which gives space for identity change on the part of the teacher, and authorizes them to do innovative teaching afterwards.

22. Option 1: Step-wise expansion of a network of participating schools, through intensive training, use of school cluster approaches, etc., with strong government support. Option 2: Compulsory universal adoption of some elements but with a step-wise component for intensified implementation to raise the proportion of schools with a quality programme. Option 3: Retention of the orthodox curriculum but with an

effort to introduce pupil activities (Sinclair, 1980).

23. Caribbean Community and Common Market.

24. The programme aimed at empowering young people with skills such as decision-making, creative thinking, critical thinking and the capacity to empathize in areas relevant to a young person's physical, emotional and social health (Mangrulkar et al., 2001, p. 40).

25. For discussion of the processes of curriculum change in conflict-affected societies and after regime change see, for example, Tawil (2001), Tawil & Harley (2004).

26. 'Learner-friendliness' refers to 'pupil-centred learning in an adequate environment which stimulates intellectual, physical, emotional and social competencies leading to the development of pupils' individual potential and of their pro-social attitudes, self-confidence and self-respect as well as respect for others' (Georgescu, 2001, p. 2).

CHAPTER VI

# Suggestions for a high-impact model

Our case studies have shown that education for peace, respect for human rights, active citizenship and health-preserving behaviours is possible but difficult. Educators have to put real will and resources into programme development in order to have a tangible and lasting impact on school programmes and on students' attitudes, values and behaviours. These lessons have been learned. Now we consider what precisely needs to be done.

The initiative to strengthen the 'learning to live together' component of schooling could come in several ways:

- A new overall national curriculum is being developed following a major political transition (e.g. initiating multi-party democracy, a peace agreement, post-conflict reconstruction).
- A new overall national curriculum is being developed, following a change in government or education minister, or the recommendations of a national commission.
- The government decides to strengthen or re-orient an existing national curriculum, specifically to introduce or strengthen coverage of education for peace, human rights, citizenship, preventive health, etc.
- Curriculum initiatives are to be undertaken on an action-research or pilot basis or by NGOs, covering a number of schools.
- Head-teacher or staff initiatives at a particular school.

Each of these scenarios will require a somewhat different approach. If there is to be a *total renewal of national curricula*, then the process begins with consensus-building on overall goals, policies and processes.[1] It will be important to include all the goals in Chapter II in the vision statement that emerges from this process, while highlighting those of special motivational force. If possible, there should also be a decision to set up a special advisory group and core team of people already committed to this work, to develop a programme focused on these special goals (which can otherwise get lost in the process of renewal of conventional school subject syllabi and textbooks).

If there is a policy decision to *strengthen the existing national curriculum* in respect of peace-building, respect for diversity, human rights, active citizenship, or HIV/AIDS prevention, then consensus-building and the creation of a core team of educators who are committed to and experienced in these fields is again important.

Programmes undertaken on a *pilot basis or by NGOs* should normally be designed to have the potential for 'scaling up'. They should utilize the type of resources that are generally available in the country, and incorporate monitoring and evaluation components, including the collection of 'baseline' data. Linkage to interested university faculty or staff of teacher training institutions for purposes of training and evaluation can help build the human resources needed for scaling up.

Programmes developed by an *individual school or teacher* can likewise be designed to serve as a training and advocacy resource for replication elsewhere.

Some elements or guidelines for a high impact, effective initiative are suggested below (see box), drawing on the findings of the present study. *All the components of the model would be necessary for an optimal result.* Issuing a policy statement is not enough, nor are the other individual actions listed below. If a government is seriously concerned about education for behavioural development and change in the areas of peace-building, citizenship, 'life skills' and preventive health, then a major and multifaceted initiative is needed.

Readers who are not currently in a position to decide on government policy can still make a contribution. By helping to build a 'critical mass' of educators and others who are knowledgeable about this area, and perhaps by undertaking pilot activities, you can influence local and national thinking. In Northern Ireland, the early experiments were small in scale and encountered problems but created the pool of concerned and experienced educators who have helped move things forward. Many of the actions noted below can be taken at the level of a school or NGO, as well as at the macro level.

For convenience and brevity, the elements are presented in the form of policy guidelines for a national government planning curriculum innovation in this area.

**Suggested policy guidelines for an integrated approach to
skills and values development for learning to live together:
including goals of peace and conflict resolution, tolerance and respect for
diversity, respect for human rights and humanitarian norms, active citizenship,
environmental sustainability, non-pressured personal relationships and
preventive health**

Element 1.   Preparatory actions: identifying national and regional human resources for start up, participatory research, feasibility studies, stakeholder consensus-building.

Element 2.   Strong government policy commitment and vision statement.

Element 3.   Creation of a core development team including committed educators who have proven skills in experiential education and in-service teacher training.

Element 4.   Creation of a coherent and progressive age-appropriate unified curriculum framework for building skills, concepts, attitudes and values related to the goals of learning to live together, including preventive health.

Element 5.   Introduction of a 'separate subject' for behavioural skills and values, with an appropriate motivational title, or series of titles, for one period a week throughout the years of schooling. This subject can be totally separate, or if necessary, an earmarked addition to an existing 'carrier' subject. It should have its own:
- Special title(s);
- Special time-slot in the timetable;
- Special active methodology;
- Special support materials based on a pedagogically sequenced curriculum;
- Specially identified and specially trained teachers;
- Special ongoing teacher support.

Element 6.   Insertion of supporting course units/lessons units into existing subjects.

Element 7.   Textbook reform to exclude harmful material and introduce positive modeling of learning to live together related to the various goals.

Element 8.   Policy of government-supported step-wise expansion of a network of participating schools and other educational institutions and programmes (pre-school, vocational, non-formal, higher education) aiming towards universal coverage without diminution of quality.[2]

Element 9.   Conflict resolution/'life-skills'/citizenship workshops for practising and trainee teachers.

Element 10.   'Whole school'and 'whole community' approach, and multiple channels of communication.

Element 11.   Research, monitoring and evaluation.

## SUPPORTIVE ACTIONS AT INTERNATIONAL LEVEL

The theme of the present study is that not enough attention and resources are
given to behavioural skills and values development for learning to live together:
for peace and conflict resolution; respect for human rights and responsibilities;
local and global citizenship; and preventive health including sexual health. Given
the pressures on educators to attend to other matters, it would be helpful if the
international community would *strengthen this field professionally,* as well as
turning up the volume of discourse. Given the high profile of terrorism and civil
conflict, as well as the millions of deaths from HIV/AIDS and the high rates of
family break-up in many societies, resource allocation to this area should not be
difficult. Some suggestions for action by agencies, donors and educators are
offered below.

*Action 1. Development of a shared and inclusive discourse on curricula for
learning to live together,* among actors in the fields of education for peace,
conflict resolution, human rights, citizenship/civics, sustainable development,
and skills-based preventive health, notably HIV/AIDS prevention. This may
include elements of a coherent but flexible generic curriculum framework, based
on pedagogically sequenced, progressive and coherent development of
appropriate skills, concepts, attitudes and values, from kindergarten to grade
twelve, and in other education programmes.

*Action 2: Development of pedagogically sequenced generic teaching/learning
materials* for schools and other educational institutions, and for training of
teachers implementing the programme. This process should draw largely on
materials already in use in the fields of education for peace, conflict resolution,
human rights, citizenship/civics, environmental sustainability, and skills-based
preventive health, notably HIV/AIDS prevention. The generic materials would
serve as resources for use in developing national programmes and should
incorporate a range of options to take account of different national and local
situations and scenarios. They should include exemplar skills and values-based
workshops suited to students in vocational/technical, non-formal and higher
education, and 'stand-alone' courses suited to youth and community groups.
Support should be provided for the trialling of draft materials in a range of
different countries and settings.[3]

*Action 3: Development of exemplar 'life-skills'-based workshops suited for pre-
service and in-service teacher training* focussed on the experiential approaches

reviewed here. This is additional to the training of specialist teachers for the use of 'separate subject' or 'carrier subject' approaches, mentioned under Action 2.[4]

*Action 4: Building expertise in research and evaluation in this area.* Expertise is needed so that new programmes begin with appropriate participative consultations and action research. Given the newness of the field, much work is needed to develop tools for formative as well as summative evaluation, in the diverse contexts found in different regions and relating to the varied thematic emphases. The experience gained in evaluation of 'life-skills' and HIV/AIDS education, especially in the USA, can be a useful input to brainstorming about methodologies in relation to the wider range of goals discussed in this study, as can the evaluations of programmes for reducing violence in inner city schools. Evaluation tools for the purposes under discussion here would need to be adapted for local use through highly participative processes, for which reason capacity-building at international and national level is critical.[5]

*Action 5: Sponsoring innovative programmes:*
Action 5.1. Identifying and supporting *existing initiatives* in various continents/regions on an action research basis, notably where there is an interest in *expanding the programme to cover the **range** of goals discussed here*, and in formative evaluation.
Action 5.2. Identifying governments that have an interest to move forward in this area, and supporting *capacity-building for local development and ownership of **high- impact** approaches*.[6]
Action 5.3. Creating a pool of ***international resource persons*** through special training programmes that upgrade national staff active in this field to the level of 'International Master Trainer'.

*Action 6. Strengthening international networking.* It is important to link educators specializing in goals and educational objectives relating to peace, human rights, local and global citizenship, as well as responsible environmental action, and preventive health including HIV/AIDS prevention. There is a wealth of experience worldwide in these various fields but it is not well-shared. One of the challenges for international action is to link and expand networks of practitioners and researchers in this field. The reader is invited to join some of them.[7]

## NOTES

1.  For example, the Department of Education and Training in Western Australia, using an 'outcomes-based approach' to curriculum renewal, developed an Overarching Statement, together with 13 Overarching Learning Outcomes, linked in various ways to Learning Area Statements and associated Learning Outcomes leading to Student Outcome Statements. See: www.eddept.wa.au/outcomes.
2.  With ongoing research-based development of diversified programmes suited to the various types of institutions including those operating under especially difficult conditions.
3.  Including the early stages of acute emergencies and linked to psycho-social needs.
4.  A further stage is to review how the themes and skills discussed in this study relate to core areas of teacher training such as classroom management, in which two-way communication, elicitive discussion involving all students, avoidance of favouritism and prejudice, gender-sensitivity, empathy, co-operation, problem-solving and sometimes negotiation are clearly needed. There is also relevance for counselling students with personal problems, preventing bullying, encouraging student participation in school management, and so on. Linkages can then be built between the workshops focused on skills for 'learning to live together', and skills needed to function well as a teacher.
5.  Some of the psychological indicators cited in research on school violence prevention are unintelligible to non-specialists, as well as being culture-specific. This is an area where collaboration between university specialists in the programme country and international specialists can be especially fruitful.
6.  A systematic approach to working with national Education Ministries, similar to that used in the Exploring Humanitarian Law project of ICRC, should be considered by major actors in this field. In particular, the shortage of international resource persons with transferable expertise and experience should be overcome through specific training programmes that upgrade national staff active in this field to the level of 'International Master Trainer', as in the ICRC programme.
7.  Even the list of relevant networks needs to be developed. Internet search tools are useful in this regard (e.g. www.google.com). See also the websites mentioned in the References section below.

REFERENCES (indicating some websites)

Aber, J.L., et al. 1998. *Resolving conflict creatively: evaluating the developmental effects of a school-based violence prevention program in neighborhood and classroom context.* New York, NY: Columbia School of Public Health. (www.esrnational.org)

Aber, J.L.; Brown, J.L.; Henrich, C.C. 1999. *Teaching conflict resolution: an effective school-based approach to violence prevention.* New York, NY: Columbia School of Public Health.

Abramson, B. 1996. *The human rights education programme: framework for curriculum development.* Geneva, Switzerland: UNHCR.

Aguilar, P. 2003. *Protective environments and education in emergencies.* New York, NY: UNICEF. (www.reliefweb.int)

Aguilar, P.; Retamal, G. 1998. *Rapid educational response in complex emergencies: a discussion document.* Hamburg, Germany: UNESCO International Institute of Education. (www.ginie.org)

AIR. 2001. *The 2000-2001 evaluation of the reading and writing for critical thinking project.* Washington, DC: American Institutes for Research.

Allard, A.; Wilson, J. 1995. *Gender dimensions: constructing interpersonal skills in the classroom.* Melbourne, Australia: Eleanor Curtain Publishing.

Anderson, M. 1999. *Do no harm: how aid can support peace—or war.* Boulder, CO: Lynne Rienner Publishers.

Archie, C. 2003. *Post-conflict peace-building in Cambodia: peace education.* (Unpublished paper.)

Arlow, M. 2001. The challenges of social inclusion in Northern Ireland: citizenship and life skills. *In:* Tawil, S., ed. *Curriculum change and social inclusion: perspectives from the Baltic and Scandinavian countries,* p. 38-43. Geneva, Switzerland: UNESCO International Bureau of Education.

Arlow, M. 2003. Northern Ireland case study. *In:* UNESCO-IBE. *Curriculum change and social cohesion in conflict-affected societies.* Geneva, Switzerland: UNESCO International Bureau of Education.

Ashton, C. 2000. *Global education project: evaluation report for second phase.* Tirana: Institute of Pedagogical Studies; Tirana: UNICEF; Toronto, Canada: International Institute of Global Education, Ontario Institute for Studies in Education, University of Toronto.

Baccino-Astrada, A. 2003. *Implementing 'Exploring Humanitarian Law' in Latin America.* Geneva, Switzerland: ICRC. (www.icrc.org)

Balasooriya, A.S. 2001. *Learning the way of peace: a teachers' guide to peace education.* New Delhi: UNESCO.

Bandura, A. 1986. *Social foundations of thought and action: a social cognitive approach*. Englewood Cliffs, NJ: Prentice Hall.

Bandura, A. 1989. Perceived self-efficacy in the exercise of control over AIDS infection. In: Mays, V.; Albee, G.W.; Schneider, S.F., eds. *Primary prevention of AIDS: psychological approaches*, p. 128–41. Newbury Park, CA: Sage.

Baxter, P. 2001. The UNHCR peace education programme: skills for life. *Forced migration review*, vol. 11, p. 28–30. (www.fmreview.org)

Beeby, C.E. 1966. *The quality of education in developing countries*. Cambridge, MA: Harvard University Press.

Benavot, A. 2002. Curricular content and societal outcomes: a critical review from comparative educational research. In: Audigier, F.; Bottani, N., eds. *Education et vivre ensemble: learning to live together and curriculum content*. Geneva, Switzerland: UNESCO International Bureau of Education; Geneva: University of Geneva; Geneva: Department of Public Instruction.

Bennett, J. 2003. *Evaluation of REFLECT for peace and reconciliation in Burundi*. London: ActionAid. (www.reflect-action.org; www.ActionAid.org)

Berman, P.; McLaughlin, M.W. 1978. *Federal programs supporting educational change: 8. Implementing and sustaining innovations*. Santa Monica, CA: Rand.

Bernbaum, M. 1999. *Weaving ties of friendship, trust and commitment to build democracy and human rights in Peru*. (erc.hrea.org/Library/research/IPEDEHP/study_english/toc.html)

Birthistle, U. 2001. Draft SCPE *evaluation report*. Belfast, UK: Council for Curriculum, Examinations and Assessment.

Birzea, C. 1996. Education in a world in transition: between post-communism and post-modernism. *Prospects,* vol. 26, p. 673–80.

Birzea, C. 2002. *Education policy in education for democratic citizenship and the management of diversity policy in South-East Europe: Stocktaking Research Project, Country report: Romania*. Vienna: South-East European Co-operation Network. (www.see-educoop.net)

Bloom, B.S. 1964. *Taxonomy of educational objectives*. New York, NY: David McKay Company Inc.

Bowers, S. 1984. *Ways and means: an approach to problem solving*. London: Kingston Friends Workshop Group.

Brady, J.P., et al. 1998. *Evaluation of the Step-by-Step Program*. Arlington, VA: American Institutes for Research.

Breines, I.; Connell, R.; Eide, I. 2000. *Male roles and masculinities: a culture of peace perspective*. Paris: UNESCO.

Bretherton, D.; Weston, J.; Zbar, V. 2002. *Peace education in a post-conflict environment: the case of Sierra Leone*. Melbourne, Australia: Curriculum Corporation.

Brown, R.J.; Turner, J.C. 2000. Inter-personal and inter-group behaviour. *In:* Turner, J.C.; Giles, H., eds. *Inter-group behaviour.* Oxford, UK: Blackwell.

Bruner, J. 1960. *The process of education.* Cambridge, MA: Harvard University Press.

Bruner, J. 1966. *Toward a theory of instruction.* Cambridge, MA: Harvard University Press.

Brunt, J. 1996. *Caring thinking: the new intelligence.* Adelaide, Australia: Flinders University. (Workshop paper.) (www.nexus.edu.au/teachstud/gat/brunt.htm)

Budiene, V. 2001. Curriculum reform in Lithuania: lessons learned. *In:* Tawil, S., ed. *Curriculum change and social inclusion: perspectives from the Baltic and Scandinavian countries.* Geneva, Switzerland: UNESCO International Bureau of Education.

Byron, I.; Rozemeijer, S. 2001. *Curriculum development for learning to live together: the Caribbean sub-region — the final report of the sub-regional seminar held in Havana, Cuba, 15-18 May 2001.* Geneva, Switzerland: UNESCO International Bureau of Education.

Bush, K.D.; Saltarelli, D. 2000. *The two faces of education in ethnic conflict: towards a peace-building education for children.* Florence, Italy: Innocenti Research Centre, UNICEF. (www.unicef.org)

CCEA. 2000. *Mutual understanding and cultural heritage: cross-curricular guidance materials.* Belfast, UK: Council for the Curriculum, Examinations and Assessment. (www.ccea.org.uk)

CDE. 2000. *Desk study on capacities and opportunities for human rights and governance awareness building in the context of the peace process in Liberia.* Monrovia: Center for Democratic Empowerment; Paris: UNESCO.

Chin, R.; Benne, K.D. 1969. General strategies for effecting change in human systems. *In:* Bennis, W.G.; Benne, K.D.; Chin, R., eds. *The planning of change.* New York, NY: Holt, Rinehart & Winston.

COE. 2000. *Training for democratic citizenship: teaching documents.* Strasbourg, France: Council of Europe.

COE. 2002. *Education for democratic citizenship 2000-2004: recommendation (2002) 12 of the Committee of Ministers to member states on education for democratic citizenship (adopted by the Committee of Ministers on 16 October 2002).* Strasbourg, France: Council of Europe.

Colbert, V.; Chiappe, C.; Arboleda, J. 1990. *The New School Programme (Escuela Nueva): more and better primary education for children in rural areas.* Bogota: UNICEF.

Connell, R. 2000. Arms and the man: using the new research on masculinity to understand violence and promote peace in the contemporary world. *In:*

Breines, I.; Connell, R.; Eide, I., eds. *Male roles and masculinities: a culture of peace perspective*. Paris: UNESCO.

Cox, C. 2002. Citizenship education in curriculum reforms of the 1990s in Latin America. *In:* Audigier, F.; Bottani, N., eds. *Education et vivre ensemble: learning to live together and curriculum content*. Geneva, Switzerland: UNESCO International Bureau of Education; Geneva: University of Geneva; Geneva: Department of Public Instruction.

Crandall, D. 1982. *People, policies and practices: examining the chain of school improvement*. Andover, MA: The Network.

CRI. 2000. *Education and the culture of democracy: early childhood practice: step by step*. Washington, DC: Children's Resources International. (www. childrensresources.org)

Crisp, J.; Talbot, C.; Cipollone, D.B. 2001. *Learning for a future: refugee education in developing countries*. Geneva, Switzerland: UNHCR. (www.unhcr.ch)

Dalin, P. 1998. Developing the twenty-first century school: a challenge to reformers. *In:* Hargreaves, A., et al. *International handbook of educational change*. London: Kluwer Academic Publishers.

Delors, J., et al. 1996. *Learning—the treasure within: report to UNESCO of the International Commission on Education for the Twenty-first Century*. Paris: UNESCO.

DENI. 1989. *EMU: a cross-curricular theme: report of the Ministerial Cross-curricular Theme Working Group on EMU*. Belfast, UK: Department of Education for Northern Ireland.

Devadoss, M. 2001. Post-conflict situations: some useful perspectives from Africa. *In: Curriculum development and education for living together: conceptual and managerial challenges in Africa*. Geneva, Switzerland: UNESCO International Bureau of Education.

Dillon, J., et al. 2001. *Mainstreaming environmental education: a report with recommendations for DFID*. Preston Montford, UK: Field Studies Council. (www.dfid.gov.uk)

Dillon, J.; Teamey, K. 2002. Re-conceptualizing environmental education: taking account of reality. *Canadian journal of science, mathematics and technology education,* vol. 2, p. 467–83.

Dorrian, A. 1999. *Peer counselling at Pietermaritzburg Girls High School, Kwazulu Natal, South Africa*. (www.peersupport.co.uk)

Duffy, T. 2000. Creating a culture of peace in Northern Ireland. *Prospects,* vol. 30, p. 15–29.

Education World. 2003. *Conflict resolution education: four approaches*. Wallingford, CT: Education World. (www.education-world.com)

Elbers, F., ed. 2000. *Human rights education resource book*. Cambridge, MA: Human Rights Education Associates. (www.hrea.org)

Elias, M.J. 2003. *Academic and social-emotional learning*. Geneva, Switzerland: UNESCO International Bureau of Education.

Eslea, M.; Smith, P.K. 1994. *Anti-bullying work in primary schools*. Sheffield, UK: University of Sheffield. (www.uclan.ac.uk/facs/science/psychol)

ESR. 2003. *About the Resolving Conflict Creatively Program*. Cambridge, MA: Educators for Social Responsibility. (www.esrnational.org)

Finkbeiner, C.; Koplin, C. 2002. A cooperative approach for facilitating intercultural education. *Reading online,* vol. 6, no. 3. (www.readingonline.org/newliteracies)

Flowers, N., et al., eds. 2000. *The human rights education handbook: effective practices for learning, action and change*. Minneapolis, MN: University of Minnesota. (www.umn.edu/humanrts)

Fountain, S. 1997. *Education for conflict resolution: a training of trainers manual*. New York, NY: UNICEF.

Fountain, S. 1999. *Peace education in UNICEF*. New York, NY: UNICEF. (www.unicef.org).

Fox, M. 2003. *Religion, spirituality and the near-death experience*. London: Routledge.

Fraser, W.J., et al. 1996. Reflections on the causes and manifestations of violence in South African schools. *Prospects,* vol. 36, p. 249–78.

Frayha, N. 2003. Education and social cohesion in Lebanon. *Prospects,* vol. 33, p. 77–88.

Gachuhi, D. 1999. *The impact of HIV/AIDS on education systems in the Eastern and Southern Africa region and the response of education systems to HIV/AIDS life skill programmes*. New York, NY: UNICEF. (www.unicef.org)

Gagliardi, R.; Mosconi, P.B. 1995. Teacher training for multicultural education in favour of democracy and sustainable development: the territorial approach. *In:* Gagliardi, R., ed. *Teacher training and multiculturalism*. Geneva, Switzerland: UNESCO International Bureau of Education.

Galtung, J. 1969. Violence, peace and peace research. *Journal of peace studies,* vol. 6, p. 167–91.

Garcia, B.; Barriga, F.D. 2002. *Psychological and pedagogical foundations of a model of civic education for children and adolescents*. (www.civnet.org)

Gardner, H. 2000. *Intelligence reframed: multiple intelligences for the twenty-first century*. New York, NY: Basic Books.

Georgescu, D. 2001. On curriculum development in Kosovo. *Development education journal,* vol. 8, no. 3.

Georgescu, D.; Palade, E. 2003. *Reshaping education for an open society in Romania 1990-2000: case studies in large-scale education reform.* Washington, DC: World Bank. (www.worldbank.org)

Gillespie, A. 2002. *Skills-based health education to prevent HIV/AIDS: the case against integration.* New York, NY: UNICEF. (www.unicef.org/programme/lifeskills/priorities/placement.html and www.unicef.org/programme/lifeskills/sitemap.html).

Goleman, D. 1995. *Emotional intelligence: why it can matter more than IQ.* New York, NY: Bantam Books.

Guimaraes, E. 1996. The school under siege: the relationship between urban environment and the education system in Rio de Janeiro. *Prospects,* vol. 36, p. 279–92.

Gupta, L. 2000. *Psycho-social assessment of displaced children exposed to war-related violence in Sierra Leone.* Freetown: Plan International. (www.reliefweb.int; www.ginie.org)

Halperin, D.S. 1997. *To live together: shaping new attitudes to peace through education.* Geneva, Switzerland: UNESCO International Bureau of Education.

Heaslip, V. 2000. *Social, Cultural and Political Education in Northern Ireland: internal evaluation of year 8 pilot.* Belfast, UK: Council for Curriculum, Examinations and Assessment.

Heyneman, S.P. 1998. *From the party/state to multi-ethnic democracy: education and its influence on social cohesion in Europe and Central Asia.* Florence, Italy: UNICEF International Child Development Centre.

Heyneman, S.P.; Todoric-Bebic, S. 2000. A renewed sense for the purposes of schooling: the challenges of education and social cohesion in Asia, Africa, Latin America, Europe and Central Asia. *Prospects,* vol. 30, p. 145–66.

Hill, B.V. 1998. Values education: the Australian experience. *Prospects,* vol. 28, p. 173–91.

Holt, J. 2001. Discovering democracy in Australia. *Prospects,* vol. 31, p. 307–18.

Hood, P.D. 1982. *The role of linking agents in school improvement: a review, analysis, and synthesis of recent major studies.* San Francisco, CA: Far West Laboratory for Educational Research and Development.

Hopkins, D. 2002. Educational innovations: generic lessons learned from (a) regional practice. *In:* Thijs, A.; de Feiter, L.; Van den Akker, J. 2002. *International learning on education reform: towards more effective ways of cooperation.* Amsterdam, Netherlands: Dutch Expertise Consortium for International Development of Education (DECIDE).

Hord, S.M. 1992. *Facilitative leadership: the imperative for change.* Austin, TX: South-West Educational Development Laboratory. (www.sedl.org/change)

ICRC. 2001. *Exploring humanitarian law: education modules for young people.* Geneva, Switzerland: International Committee of the Red Cross and Red Crescent.

INEE. 2002. *Peace Education Programme: resource materials.* Paris: Inter-agency Network for Education in Emergencies; Geneva, Switzerland: UNHCR. (www.ineesite.org)

IRC. 2003. *IRC psycho-social teacher training guide.* New York, NY: International Rescue Committee.

Isaacs, A. 2002. *Education, conflict and peace-building: a diagnostic tool.* Ottawa: CIDA.

ISCA. 1996. *Promoting psycho-social well-being among children affected by armed conflict and displacement: principles and approaches.* Geneva, Switzerland: International Save the Children Alliance.

Johannessen, E. 2002. *Evaluation of human rights education in southern Caucasus.* Oslo: Norwegian Refugee Council.

Joyce, B.; Showers, B. 1980. Improving in-service training: the message of research. *Educational leadership,* vol. 37, p. 375–85.

Kalichman, S.; Hospers, H. 1997. Efficacy of behavioural-skills enhancement HIV risk reduction interventions in community settings. *AIDS,* vol. 11A, S. 191–99.

Kann, L., et al. 1995. The school health policies and programs study: rationale for a nationwide status report on school health. *Journal of school health,* vol. 65, p. 291–94.

Kennedy, K. Undated. Civics education for the 'techno' generation: what should we expect young people to know and be able to do as future citizens? *Ethos 7-12,* vol. 8, no. 2, term 2.

Kennedy, K.; Mellor, S. 2000. *Reviving civics education for a new agenda in Australia: the contribution of the IEA study.* Canberra, Australia: University of Canberra. (www.canberra.edu.au/civics/papers/reviving_civics.html)

Keogh, H. 2003. Learning for citizenship in Ireland: the role of adult education. *In:* Medel-Anonuevo, C.; Mitchell, G., eds. 2003. *Citizenship, democracy and lifelong learning,* p. 1–42. Hamburg, Germany: UNESCO Institute for Education.

Kerr, D. 2002. *Assessment and evaluation in citizenship education.* London: National Foundation for Educational Research. (www.britishcouncil.org.uk)

King, R. 1999. *Sexual behaviour change for HIV: where have the theories taken us?* Geneva, Switzerland: UNAIDS. (www.unaids.org)

Kirby, D., et al. 1994. School based programs to reduce sexual risk behaviours: a review of effectiveness. *Public health reports,* vol. 109, p. 339–61.

Kline, R. 2000. A model for improving rural schools: Escuela Nueva in Colombia and Guatemala. *Current issues in comparative education,* vol. 2, no. 2. (www.tc.columbia.edu/cice/articles)

Lebmann, S. 2002. Databases on human rights education. *International review of education,* vol. 48, p. 287–92.

Lederach, J.P. 1994. *Preparing for peace: conflict transformation across cultures.* Syracuse, NY: Syracuse University Press.

Lewin, K. 1936. *Principles of topological psychology.* New York, NY: McGraw-Hill.

Lipman, M. 1995. Caring as thinking. *Inquiry,* vol. 15, no. 1.

Lipman, M. 2003. *Thinking in education.* Cambridge, UK: Cambridge University Press.

Lohrenscheit, C. 2002. International approaches in human rights education. *International review of education,* vol. 48, p. 173–85.

Lorenzo, A.D. 2003. *Learning peace: UNHCR's peace education program in refugee camps in Kenya.* New York, NY: Internet Forum on Conflict Prevention, UN Office for Coordination of Humanitarian Assistance. (www.preventconflict.org/ifcp)

McBer, H. 2000. *Research into teacher effectiveness: a model of teacher effectiveness.* London: Department for Education and Employment. (www.dfes.gov.uk)

McCallin, M. 1996. *The psycho-social well-being of refugee children.* Geneva, Switzerland: International Catholic Child Bureau.

McCauley, C. 2002. Head-first versus feet-first in peace education. *In:* Salomon, G.; Nevo, B., eds. *Peace education around the world: the concept, the practice, the research.* Mahwah, NJ: Lawrence Earlbaum Associates. (www.peace.ca)

Machel, G. 1996. *The impact of armed conflict on children.* New York, NY: United Nations. (www.unicef.org).

Machel, G. 2001. *The impact of war on children: a review of progress since the 1996 UN report on the Impact of Armed Conflict on Children.* London: Hurst.

McKeown, R. Undated. *Education for sustainable development toolkit.* (www.esdtoolkit.org)

Macksoud, M. 1993. *Helping children cope with the stresses of war: a manual for parents and teachers.* New York, NY: UNICEF.

Mangrulkar, L.; Whitman, C.V.; Posner, M. 2001. *Life skills approach to child and adolescent healthy human development.* Washington, DC: Pan American Health Organisation. (www.paho.org)

Mannah, S. 2002. South Africa: the complex role of teaching about HIV/AIDS in schools. *Prospects,* vol. 32, p. 155–70.

Maoz, I. 2002. Conceptual mapping and evaluation of peace education programs: the case of education for coexistence through inter-group encounters between Jews and Arabs in Israel. *In:* Salomon, G.; Nevo, B., eds. *Peace education around the world: the concept, the practice, the research.* Mahwah, NJ: Lawrence Earlbaum Associates. (www.peace.ca)

Meyer-Bisch, P., ed. 1995. *Culture of democracy: a challenge for schools.* Paris: UNESCO.

Midttun, E. 1999. *Concept paper on human rights education.* Oslo: Norwegian Refugee Council.

Miller,V.W.; Affolter, F.W. 2002. *Helping children outgrow war.* Washington, DC: USAID.

Mitchell, G. 2003. Inter-cultural education for democracy: the case of South Africa. *In:* Medel-Anonuevo, C.; Mitchell, G., eds. *Citizenship, democracy and lifelong learning,* p. 153–67. Hamburg, Germany: UNESCO Institute for Education.

Mockus, A. 2002. Co-existence as harmonization of law, morality and culture. *Prospects,* vol. 121, p. 19–38.

Mulder, B. 1997. *Moral development's development: recent research.* (www.hope.edu/academic/psychology/335/webrep/moraldev.htlm)

Nevo, B.; Brem, I. 2002. Peace education programs and the evaluation of their effectiveness. *In:* Salomon, G.; Nevo, B., eds. 2002. *Peace education around the world: the concept, the practice, the research.* Mahwah, NJ: Lawrence Earlbaum Associates. (www.peace.ca)

NICC. 1990. *Cross-curricular themes: guidance materials.* Belfast, UK: Northern Ireland Curriculum Council.

NICED. 1989. *EMU: a planning guide for teachers.* Belfast, UK: Northern Ireland Council for Educational Development.

Nicolai, S. 2003. *Psycho-social needs of conflict-affected children and adolescents.* Paris: UNESCO International Institute for Educational Planning. (Introductory paper for IIEP/World Bank Summer School on Post-conflict Reconstruction in the Education Sector.)

Nicolai, S.; Triplehorn, C. 2003. *The role of education in protecting children in conflict.* London: Department for International Development.

Northern Ireland. Department of Education. 2000. *Report of a survey of provision for Education for Mutual Understanding in post-primary schools.* Belfast, UK: Department of Education. (www.deni.gov.uk/inspection)

Obura, A. 2002. *UNHCR Peace Education Programme: evaluation report.* Geneva, Switzerland: UNHCR. (www.unhcr.ch)

OHCHR. Undated. *ABC Teaching human rights: practical activities for primary and secondary schools.* Geneva, Switzerland: Office of the High Commissioner for Human Rights. (www.unhchr.ch)

Ohsako, T. 1997. *Violence at school: global issues and interventions*. Paris: UNESCO.

Oliver, C.; Candappa, M. 2003. *Tackling bullying: listening to the views of children and young people*. London: Department for Education and Science.

Olsholt, O. 2001. *Philosophy for children: a Norwegian approach*. Oslo: University of Oslo, International Conference on Philosophy in Society.

Olweus, D. 1996. Bully/victim problems in school. *Prospects*, vol. 36, p. 331–60.

O'Neill, J. 1993. *Quaker Peace Education Project Evaluation: final report*. Belfast, UK: Charities Evaluation Service.

Payton, J.W., et al. 2000. Social and emotional learning: a framework for promoting mental health and reducing risk behaviours in children and youth. *Journal of school health*, vol. 70, p. 179–85. (www.casel.org)

Peace Corps. 2001. *Life skills manual*. Washington, DC: Peace Corps.

Pettigrew, T.F. 1998. Inter-group contact theory. *In:* Spence, J.T.; Darley, J.M.; Foss, D.J., eds. *Annual review of psychology*, vol. 49, p. 65–85.

Pike, G.; Selby, D. 1988. *Global teacher, global learner*. London: Hodder & Stoughton.

Pike, G.; Selby, D. Undated. *Global education: making basic learning a child-friendly experience*. Amman: UNICEF; Toronto, Canada: International Institute of Global Education, Ontario Institute for Studies in Education, University of Toronto.

Pingel, F. 1999. *UNESCO guidebook on textbook research and textbook revision*. Paris: UNESCO; Braunschweig: Georg Eckert Institute for International Textbook Research.

Power, F.C.; Higgins, A.; Kohlberg, L. 1989 *Lawrence Kohlberg's approach to moral education*. New York, NY: Columbia University Press.

Power, F.C. 1999. Education toward democracy: how can it be accomplished? *Prospects*, vol. 29, p. 217–22.

Pozniak, S. 2003. Training teachers for citizenship education. *In:* Medel-Anonuevo, C.; Mitchell, G., eds. *Citizenship, democracy and lifelong learning*. Hamburg, Germany: UNESCO Institute for Education.

Psacharopoulus, G.; Rojas, C.; Velez, E. 1993 Achievement evaluation of Colombia's Escuela Nueva: is multigrade the answer? *Comparative education review*, vol. 37, no. 3.

Pupovci, D.; Taylor, A. 2003. *Reading and writing for critical thinking: evaluation report*. Prishtina: Kosova Education Centre. (www.see-educoop.net)

Puig, J. 1995. *La educación moral en la enseñanza obligatoria*. Barcelona, Spain: Horsori.

Rambo, L. 1993. *Understanding religious conversion.* New Haven, CT: Yale University Press.

Raths, L.; Harmin, M.; Simon, S. 1966. *Values and teaching.* Columbus, OH: CE Merrill.

Reardon, B. 1997. *Tolerance: the threshold of peace.* Paris: UNESCO.

Reardon, B. 2001. *Education for a culture of peace in a gender perspective.* Paris: UNESCO.

Reardon, B.; Cabezudo, A. 2002. *Learning to abolish war: teaching toward a culture of peace.* New York, NY: Hague Appeal for Peace.

Remedia Trust. Undated. UNESCO *project on life skills in non-formal education.* New Delhi: Remedia Trust. (www.unicef.org)

Renwick, W.L. 1998. Clarence Edward Beeby. *Prospects,* vol. 28, p. 335–48.

Retamal, G. 2000. *Building a rapid educational response in Sierra Leone.* Hamburg, Germany: UNESCO Institute of Education. (www.ginie.org)

Retamal, G.; Aedo-Richmond, R., eds. 1998. *Education as a humanitarian response.* London: Cassell.

Rhodes, R.; Walker, D.; Martor, N. 1998. *Where do our girls go?: female dropout in the IRC-Guinea primary schools.* New York, NY: International Rescue Committee.

Ritzen, J.; Woolcock, M. 2000. *Social cohesion, public policy and economic growth: implications for countries in transition.* Washington, DC: World Bank. (www.worldbank.org)

Rogers, E.M. 1995. *Diffusion of innovations.* 4th ed. New York, NY: The Free Press.

Rosenberg, M. 1999. Non-violent communication. Encinitas, CA: Puddledancer Press. (www.spiritsite.com)

Rugh, A.; Bossert, H. 1998. *Involving communities in the delivery of education programs.* Washington, DC: Creative Associates. (www.worldbank.org)

Ruiz, R.O. 1998. Indiscipline or violence: the problem of bullying in school. *Prospects,* vol. 28, p. 587–99.

Salmi, J. 2000. *Violence, democracy and education: an analytical framework.* Washington, DC: World Bank.

Salomon, G. 2002 The nature of peace education: not all programmes are created equal. *In:* Salomon, G.; Nevo, B., eds. *Peace education around the world: the concept, the practice, the research.* Mahwah, NJ: Lawrence Earlbaum Associates. (www.peace.ca)

Salomon, G. 2003. *Does peace education make a difference?* Haifa, Israel: University of Haifa Centre for Research on Peace Education. (Draft.) (www.construct.haifa.ac.il)

Salomon, G.; Nevo, B., eds. 2002. *Peace education around the world: the concept, the practice, the research.* Mahwah, NJ. Lawrence Earlbaum Associates. (www.peace.ca)

Schaalma, H.P., et al. 2002. HIV education for young people: intervention effectiveness, programme development and future research. *Prospects,* vol. 32, no. 2.

Schugurensky, D. 2002. *Colombia's Escuela Nueva.* Toronto, Canada: Ontario Institute for Studies in Education, University of Toronto.

Sharp, S.; Thompson, D.A.; Arora, C.M.J. 2002. *Bullying: effective strategies for long-term change.* London: Routledge/Falmer.

Simon, S.B.; Howe, L.; Kirschenbaum, H. 1972. *Values clarification: a handbook for practical strategies for teachers and students.* New York, NY: Hart Publishing.

Sinclair, M. 1980. *School and community in the Third World.* London: Croom Helm.

Sinclair, M. 2001. Education in emergencies. In: Crisp, J.; Talbot, C.; Cipollone, D., eds. *Learning for a future: refugee education in developing countries.* Geneva, Switzerland: UNHCR. (www.unhcr.ch).

Sinclair, M. 2002. *Planning education in and after emergencies.* Paris: UNESCO International Institute of Educational Planning. (www. unesco.org/iiep)

Skilbeck, M. 1976. Education and cultural change. *Compass: journal of the Irish Association for Curriculum Development,* vol. 5, no. 2.

Slavin, R.E. 1998. Sand, bricks and seeds: school change strategies and readiness for reform. In: Hargreaves, A., et al., eds. *International handbook of educational change.* London: Kluwer Academic Publishers.

Smith, A.; Dunn, S. 1990. *Extending inter-school links: an evaluation of contact between Protestant and Catholic pupils in Northern Ireland.* Coleraine, UK: Centre for the Study of Conflict, University of Ulster.

Smith, A.; Fountain, S.; McLean, H. 2002. *Civic education in primary and secondary schools in the Republic of Serbia.* Belgrade: UNICEF. (In collaboration with UNESCO, Open Society Institute, Fund for an Open Society, Serbia.) (www.see-educoop.net)

Smith, A.; Montgomery, A. 1997. *Values in education in Northern Ireland.* (http://cain.ulst.ac.uk)

Smith, A.; Robinson, A. 1996. *Education for Mutual Understanding: the initial statutory years.* Coleraine, UK: Centre for the Study of Conflict, University of Ulster.

Smith, A.; Vaux, T. 2002. *Education, conflict and international development.* London: Department for International Development.

Smith, D.; Stephenson, P. 1991. Why some schools don't have bullies. *In:* Elliot, M., ed. *Bullying: a practical guide to coping for schools.* Harlow, UK: Longman.

Smith, P.; Samara, M. 2003. *Evaluation of the DfES anti-bullying pack.* London: Department for Education and Science. (www.dfes.gov.uk/research)

Sommers, M. 2001. Peace education and refugee youth. *In:* Crisp, J.; Talbot, C.; Cipollone, D., eds. *Learning for a future: refugee education in developing countries,* p. 163–216. Geneva, Switzerland: UNHCR. (www.unhcr.ch)

Sommers, M. 2002. *Children, education and war: reaching Education for All (EFA) objectives in countries affected by conflict.* Washington, DC: Conflict Prevention and Reconstruction Unit, World Bank. (www.worldbank.org).

Soule, S. 2001. *Research verifies success of Center programmes.* Calabasas, CA: Center for Civic Education. (www.civnet.org)

Spajic-Vrkas, V. 2002. *Education policy in education for democratic citizenship and the management of diversity in South-East Europe: Stocktaking Research Project, Country Report—Croatia.* Vienna: South-East European Co-operation Network. (www.see-educoop.net)

Steele, J.L. 2000. The Reading and Writing for Critical Thinking Project: a framework for school change. *In:* Klooster, D.J.; Steele, J.L.; Bloem, P.L., eds. *Ideas without boundaries: international education reform through reading and writing for critical thinking.* Washington, DC: International Reading Association. (www.readingonline.org)

Stromquist, N.P.; Vigil, J.D. 1996. Violence in schools in the United States of America: trends, causes and responses. *Prospects,* vol. 26, no. 2.

Talbot, C.; Muigai, K. 1998. Environmental education for refugees: guidelines, implementation and lessons learned. In: Retamal, G.; Aedo-Richmond, R., eds. *Education as a humanitarian response,* p. 223–47. London: Cassell.

Tawil, S., ed. 1997. *Final report on case studies of the workshop on educational destruction and reconstruction in disrupted societies.* Geneva: UNESCO International Bureau of Education.

Tawil, S. 2000. International humanitarian law and basic education. *International review of the Red Cross,* vol. 82, p. 581–600. (www.icrc.org)

Tawil, S., ed. 2001. *Curriculum change and social inclusion: perspectives from the Baltic and Scandinavian countries.* Geneva, Switzerland: UNESCO International Bureau of Education.

Tawil, S.; Azami-Tawil, B. 2001. *Combating discrimination: what role for the Red Cross?* Geneva, Switzerland: International Federation of the Red Cross and Red Crescent Societies.

Tawil, S.; Harley, A., eds. 2004. *Education, conflict and social cohesion.* Geneva, Switzerland: UNESCO International Bureau of Education.

Taylor, M. 1993. *Values education in Europe. Vol. 8: A comparative overview of a survey of 26 countries in 1993.* London: National Foundation for Educational Research; Paris: UNESCO.

Thorne, S. 1995. Children's rights and the listening school: an approach to counter bullying among primary school pupils. *In:* Osler, A.; Rathenow, H.; Starkey, H., eds. *Teaching for citizenship in Europe.* Stoke-on-Trent, UK: Trentham Books.

Tibbitts, F. 1997a. *A primer for selecting democratic and human rights education teaching materials.* New York, NY: Open Society Institute; Cambridge, MA: Human Rights Education Associates. (www.hrea.org)

Tibbitts, F. 1997b. *Case studies in human rights education: examples from Central and Eastern Europe.* Strasbourg, France: Council of Europe. (www.hrea.org)

Tibbitts, F. 1999. *Impact of human rights related curriculum in Romania.* Cambridge, MA: Human Rights Education Associates. (www.hrea.org)

Tibbitts, F. 2002. Understanding what we do: emerging models for human rights education. *International review of education,* vol. 48, p. 159–71.

Tibbitts, F.; Torney-Purta, J. 1999. *Citizenship education in Latin America: preparing for the future.* Cambridge, MA: Human Rights Education Associates.

Titus, D.N. 1994. *Values education in American secondary schools.* Kutztown, PA: Kutztown University Conference. (www.hi-ho.ne.jp/taku77/refer/titus.htm)

Tolfree, D. 1996. *Restoring playfulness: different approaches to assisting children who are psychologically affected by war or displacement.* Stockholm: Swedish Save the Children.

Torney-Purta, J., et al. 2001. *Citizenship and education in twenty-eight countries: civic knowledge and engagement at age fourteen.* Amsterdam, Netherlands: International Association for the Evaluation of Educational Attainments (IEA).

Trajkowski, I. 2002. *Education for democratic citizenship and the management of diversity policies in South-East Europe: Stocktaking Research Project, Country Report – The Republic of Macedonia.* Skopje: Skopje University/South-East European Co-operation Network. (www.see-educoop.net)

Trevaskis, D.K. 1994. *Mediation in the schools: ERIC digest.* Bloomington, IN: ERIC Clearinghouse for Social Studies/Social Studies Education. (www.ericfacility.net)

Triplehorn, C. 2002. *Guidance notes for education in emergencies.* (www.ineesite.org).

Tyrrell, J. 1995. *Quaker Peace Education Project 1988-1994: developing untried strategies*. Coleraine, UK: Centre for the Study of Conflict, University of Ulster.

UNAIDS. 1997. *Impact of HIV and sexual health education on the sexual behaviour of young people: a review update*. Geneva, Switzerland: UNAIDS.

UNESCO. 1992. *Guidelines for curriculum and textbook development in international education*. Paris: UNESCO.

UNESCO. 1997a. *Education for all for learning to live together: contents and learning strategies—problems and solutions*. Geneva, Switzerland: UNESCO International Bureau of Education.

UNESCO. 1997b. *UNESCO and a culture of peace: promoting a global movement*. Paris: UNESCO.

UNESCO. 1998. *All human beings: a manual for human rights education*. Paris: UNESCO.

UNESCO. 2002a. *Teaching and learning for a sustainable future: a multimedia teacher education programme*. Paris: UNESCO.

UNESCO. 2002b. *Learning to be: a holistic and integrated approach to values education for human development*. Bangkok: UNESCO Regional Office for Asia and the Pacific.

UNESCO. 2002c. *Framework for action on values education in early childhood*. Paris: UNESCO.

UNESCO. 2003a. *Non-violent conflict resolution in and out of school: some examples*. Paris: UNESCO.

UNESCO. 2003b. *Learning to live together: have we failed?* Geneva, Switzerland: UNESCO International Bureau of Education.

UNESCO; KCHR. 2003. *Second step for human rights education*. Paris: UNESCO; Pristina: Kosova Centre for Human Rights.

UNICEF. 2000. *Working paper: curriculum*. New York, NY: UNICEF. (www.unicef.org)

UNICEF. 2003. *Assessment of the HIV/AIDS component of SHAPE (school-based healthy living and HIV/AIDS prevention education)*. Yangon: UNICEF. (www.unicef.org)

USAID. 2002. *Tips for developing life-skills curricula for HIV prevention among African youth: a synthesis of emerging lessons*. Washington, DC: USAID Bureau for Africa. (www.unicef.org)

Valdmaa, S. 2002. Developing civic education in Estonia. *In:* Tawil, S., ed. *Curriculum change and social inclusion: perspectives from the Baltic and Scandinavian countries*. Geneva, Switzerland: UNESCO International Bureau of Education.

Vilaca, M.T.; Sequeira, M. Undated. *A leading intervention program of primary prevention of HIV infection and AIDS in compulsory education.* (http://archive.concord.org/intl/cbe/pdf/vilaca_sequeira.pdf)

Villegas-Reimers, E. 1994. *Civic education in the school system of Latin America and the Caribbean.* Washington, DC: USAID.

Vygotsky, L.S. 1978. *Mind in society.* Cambridge, MA: Harvard University Press.

Warwick, I., et al. 2002. *The Sex and Relationship Education (SRE) Teaching Pilot: an investigation of key stakeholder perceptions.* London: Thomas Coram Research Unit, Institute of Education, University of London. (www.dfes.gov.uk/research)

Watling, R. 2001. *SCPE project external evaluation.* Leicester, UK: Centre for Citizenship Studies, University of Leicester.

Weare, K.; Gray, G. 2003. *What works in developing children's emotion and social competence and well-being?* Southampton, UK: University of Southampton. (www.dfes.gov.uk)

WEF. 2000a. *Education for All 2000 assessment: framework for action.* Paris: International Consultative Forum on Education for All, UNESCO. (www.unesco.org)

WEF. 2000b. *Thematic study: education in situations of emergency and crisis.* Paris: International Consultative Forum on Education for All, UNESCO. (www.unesco.org)

Weil, P. 2002. *The art of living in peace: guide to education for a culture of peace.* Paris: UNESCO.

Whitman, C.V.; Aldinger, C. 2002. *Skills-based health education including life-skills.* New York, NY: UNICEF; Geneva, Switzerland: World Health Organization. (Draft.)

WHO. 1997. *Life-skills education in schools.* Geneva, Switzerland: World Health Organization.

WHO. 2003a. *Skills for health: skills-based health education including life-skills: an important component of a child-friendly/health-promoting school.* Geneva, Switzerland: World Health Organization.

WHO. 2003b. *Creating an environment for emotional and social well-being: an important responsibility of a health-promoting and child friendly school.* Geneva, Switzerland: World Health Organization.

WHO; UNESCO. 1994. *School health education to prevent AIDS and STD: a resource package for curriculum planners.* Geneva, Switzerland: World Health Organization/UNESCO. (Re-issued by UNAIDS, Geneva.)

WHO; UNICEF. 1994. *The development and dissemination of life-skills education: an overview.* Geneva: World Health Organization; New York, NY: UNICEF.

World Bank. 2003. *Education and HIV/AIDS: a sourcebook of HIV/AIDS prevention programmes*. Washington, DC: World Bank.

Yohji, M. 1996. Bullying as a contemporary behaviour problem in the context of increasing 'societal privatization' in Japan. *Prospects,* vol. 36, p. 311–30.